Teaching the Art of Literature

Teaching the Art of Literature

Bruce E. Miller
State University of New York at Buffalo

National Council of Teachers of English
1111 Kenyon Road, Urbana, Illinois 61801

To Thea Maronian

Grateful acknowledgment is made for permission to reprint the following material: "When You Are Old," copyright 1906 by Macmillan Publishing Co., Inc., renewed 1934 by William Butler Yeats. "The Fallow Deer at the Lonely House," from *The Complete Poems of Thomas Hardy* edited by James Gibson (New York: Macmillan, 1978). "Song of Myself" (number 11) from the book *Leaves of Grass* by Walt Whitman. Reprinted by permission of Doubleday & Company, Inc.

Book Design: Tom Kovacs, interior; V. Martin, cover

NCTE Stock Number 51922

It is the policy of NCTE in its journals and other publications to provide a forum for the open discussion of ideas concerning the content and the teaching of English and the language arts. Publicity accorded to any particular point of view does not imply endorsement by the Executive Committee, the Board of Directors, or the membership at large, except in announcements of policy where such endorsement is clearly specified.

Library of Congress Cataloging in Publication Data

Miller, Bruce E
   Teaching the art of literature.

   Includes bibliographical references.
   1. Literature—Study and teaching. I. Title.
PN59.M54   807   80-20673
ISBN 0-8141-5192-2

Contents

Acknowledgments

Certain parts of this book have been printed elsewhere in somewhat different form. The first paragraph and a few sentences of Chapter II first appeared in *Creative Dramatics in the Language Arts Classroom: Report of the Second Annual Conference on Language Arts, State University of New York at Buffalo* (1976), 83–90; all of Chapter VI was first printed in *Journal of English Teaching Techniques*, 6, No. 3 (Fall 1973); the first half of Chapter VIII originally appeared in *Illinois Quarterly*, 34, No. 1 (September 1971), 55–64. I am grateful to the editors of these journals for allowing me to try out some of my ideas in their pages.

Introduction

This book is divided into two sections. The first section describes the nature of literary experience and the kinds of approaches that different readers take to literature in order to attain that experience. The second section applies this background to the teaching of specific works. In the selection of those works, I have made the inevitable compromise between the wish to get some degree of generic spread and the wish to share with my readers the works that I love best. The book examines no contemporary literature but I have no prejudice against it, either in itself or its inclusion in the curriculum. I omitted samples of contemporary writing merely because they were superseded by works I preferred or by the requirement I imposed on myself to provide some variety in the types.

The approach to teaching literature that is offered here is mainly based on two assumptions; one about the character of literature and another about the connection between reading literature and teaching it. The one assumption is that literature is an art, which at first glance may appear tame enough, nothing more than a platitude indeed. But much, perhaps most, of the teaching of literature that goes on in high schools and also in colleges proceeds from an assumption that is different from this and, finally, incompatible with it. That contrary assumption is that literature is one of the humanities.

A conventional distinction between arts and humanities puts painting and other graphics, dance, music, architecture, and sculpture among the arts, and places philosophy and most of the social sciences, including social criticism, among the humanities. Literature and drama hang ambiguously between. On this classification, the characteristic that seems to distinguish the arts from the humanities is that, in art, the attention of the audience is centered upon just one object which is intended completely to fill and even overwhelm the mind—whereas, in the humanities, a communication is designed to stimulate reflection and then to direct that reflection out upon the world. Thus we "attend to" Mozart's overture to *Figaro,* but we "think about" Plato's *Phaedo.* There is more than this to the difference between the arts and humanities, but this much at least seems basic and open to general agreement.

With respect to literature, including drama, the question is not what *is* it, an art or a humanity. Obviously it *can* be either the one or the other, since some people read literature in order to experience a concrete object and others read it in order to reflect upon the world. The question to ask, rather, is what *should* it be. Good arguments exist on either side of the question, but the ones I find most persuasive are on the side of reading literature as an art. One of these arguments is negative, against taking literature as one of the humanities; the other argument is positive, for reading it as art.

In a nutshell, the negative argument is that, as one of the humanities, literature offers very little. Humanistic writing is always a message that gives us ideas, as *Phaedo* conveys ideas about the immortality of the soul which have to be taken very seriously. We expect Plato, Emerson, and such a modern reflective writer as David Riesman to give us ideas that we shall consider, accept or reject, and use to help us to understand our world. Now, what happens if we try this same approach to great literature? What messages, what ideas about the world, do we get from Chaucer, Shakespeare, Milton, Browning? Here is Chaucer:

> And lightly as it comes, so will we spend.
>
> *(Pardoner's Tale,* 453)

(Paraphrase: Easy come, easy go.) Here is Shakespeare:

> The readiness is all.
>
> *(Hamlet,* V, ii, 232)

(Once you have prepared yourself for an event, there is nothing more that you can do.) Here is Milton:

> So dear to Heaven is saintly chastity,
> That when a soul is found sincerely so,
> A thousand liveried angels lackey her,
> Driving far off each thing of sin and guilt.
>
> *(Comus,* 453–456)

(Heaven assists virtue.) Or, finally, here is Browning, perhaps the one English poet who most employs abstract ideas:

> Oh, the little more, and how much it is!
> And the little less, and what worlds away!
>
> ("By the Fireside," XXIX)

(Sometimes even a great deal is not enough.)

Now, could anyone call these lines Great Ideas of Western Man or Thoughts to Live By? Has anyone ever found in a great poet or fiction writer a generalization about the world that he could not have acquired more readily, more accurately, and more fully from some other source? Things that are good for one purpose may not be good for another. We do not bail out a boat with a teaspoon nor swat flies with a tennis racket. Neither should we go to literature to get what is better provided elsewhere— namely, generalizations about ourselves and the world.

On the other hand, we know that literature deals with meaning. There is no contradiction here as long as we realize that meaning, genuine significance, can inhere in things other than the explicit and literal messages that the humanities employ. A descending seventh in music, a concentration of dental consonants in poetry, a balance or imbalance of masses in architecture can all have meaning. Indeed, the meanings that art can convey are different from those that are capable of expression in philosophy, sociology, and the other humanities. Thus, one who wants to become familiar with the notion that God is totally in act had better read philosophy—Aristotle and Aquinas both deal with the idea—but one who wants to know the consequences of the intuition that God loves humans will do better to turn from philosophy to art—to the Psalms or to "He's Got the Whole World in His Hand" or to Giotto's *Christ Entering Jerusalem*.

The foregoing comparison suggests the positive argument for reading literature as art. Not everything that is meant can also be said in the form of abstract language, and art is better equipped than the humanities to convey certain meanings. Whenever we use the word *meaning* or its derivatives and synonyms, we can have two very different things in mind. When we say to a student, for example, "The meaning is not clear in this sentence," we have one thing in mind; when we say to a friend, "Your gift was full of meaning for me," we have something else in mind. The difference is basically a distinction between words on the one hand and events on the other. We say of both messages and events that they "mean" or are "meaningful" or have "meaning," but we do not think, therefore, that they mean the same thing or are meaningful in the same way.

The difference between the meaningfulness of words and the meaningfulness of events can be seen in the development of the figure of Polonius in *Hamlet*. Here are some familiar lines from Polonius's speech of advice to his son Laertes, who is about to go to France:

> Beware
> Of entrance to a quarrel, but, being in,
> Bear 't that th' opposed may beware of thee.
> Give each man thine ear, but few thy voice;
> Take each man's censure, but reserve thy judgment.
> Costly thy habit as thy purse can buy,
> But not express'd in fancy; rich, not gaudy;
> For the apparel oft proclaims the man,
> And they in France of the best rank and station

Are most select and generous, chief in that.
Neither a borrower, nor a lender be;
For loan oft loses both itself and friend,
And borrowing dulls the edge of husbandry.
This above all: to thine own self be true,
And it must follow, as the night the day,
Thou canst not then be false to any man.

(I, iii, 65–80)

When we respond to these lines as a form of words, we take them first as a set of problems in translation. Thus, in the fourth line down, we realize that the words are not to be taken in an exactly literal sense; we decode the expression "Give each man thine ear" as "Listen to everyone," and the phrase "but few thy voice" we expand into "but do not offer your advice to many people." Then we understand that the next line is a paraphrase of the one we have just translated and that therefore the word *censure* cannot mean here quite the same thing that it ordinarily means to us.

After translating or decoding words we often act on them further by generalizing them or—the opposite—by applying them to specific circumstances. We would be generalizing this passage, for instance, if we were to say, "Polonius is recommending prudence or thoughtful caution as a basis for dealing with others," and we would be specifying the passage if we were to say, "I won't buy that coat with the fur collar and cuffs after all, because although it is good-looking it is too showy for me." In addition, we can give an opinion about a passage; most readers would agree, for instance, that this speech by Polonius is both sententious in its form and wise, or at least worldly-wise, in its substance.

As we go on reading the play and we hear Polonius speak in different contexts, this early speech to his son recurs to us, and we begin to respond to it in a new way. We next see him in the second act, speaking first to his servant Reynaldo, whom he is sending to Paris to give Laertes some money and also to investigate Laertes's behavior. Polonius now appears in a somewhat different light: Though still the loving father, he also reveals himself to be the cynical man of the world. He assumes that Laertes has employed his freedom to get into at least minor scrapes, and he wants to find out what these mischiefs are. He orders Reynaldo to sound out Parisian acquaintances of Laertes by dropping hints that Laertes has indulged in such indiscretions as

... drinking, fencing, swearing, quarrelling,
Drabbing, you may go so far.

(II, ii, 25–26)

The acquaintances' response to these charges will give Polonius all the information he needs in order to learn how Laertes is conducting himself.

Then, after dismissing Reynaldo, Polonius turns to his daughter Ophelia, who tells him of Hamlet's distraught behavior toward her, and again Polonius acts like a man of the world, presuming that Hamlet's sexual frustration is the cause of his supposed insanity. We confirm our insight that Polonius is a highly successful and capable man of affairs when, hurrying off to the king and queen to give them his diagnosis of Hamlet's illness, he reinforces his argument by asking,

> Hath there been such a time,—I'd fain know that,—
> That I have positively said, " 'Tis so,"
> When it prov'd otherwise?

> (II, ii, 153–155)

The king, who obviously respects Polonius, answers briefly, "Not that I know."

But just as soon as we have formed one distinct and favorable opinion of Polonius, a different interpretation of his character begins to suggest itself. Already we have heard the queen complain that he talks too much—"More matter with less art," she asks (II, ii, 96)—and soon after, when the players come, Hamlet ridicules him and betrays him into making a fool of himself. Our picture of Polonius is advanced when Hamlet tells the players to let Polonius show them their accommodations and warns them, "and look you mock him not" (II, ii 549–550). Now we realize what Polonius's condition is. He is a superannuated civil servant, hovering in a vacuum between past solid achievement and the silliness of approaching senility. He mixes the cunning of an experienced high-level administrator with the blundering of a vain old man. Thus Hamlet is both contemptuous of Polonius—he ridicules him—but also protective—he guards him against others' ridicule that might be more hurtful.

In these first two acts of the play, our conception of Polonius has been steadily growing, while becoming more and more complex. First we see him as a wise and respected senior counselor, then as a scheming conniver who habitually thinks the worst, even of his son, and then as an old fool. Up to this point we have been responding mostly to words—to Polonius's words to others and theirs to him. But our conclusive impression of Polonius, the impression that governs and modifies the others, results from an action: Polonius hides behind a curtain to spy on Hamlet, and Hamlet, fearing that he is about to be assassinated, kills him. That action is very meaningful, for it concentrates in a single event all our intuitions about the man. It presents to us the suspicious cynic who supposes that he must eavesdrop to get the real truth; it presents the bungling meddler who never gets anything quite right, not even his own plots. But also it presents the man of action who, though decayed and ineffective, nevertheless really attempts to deal with the world head-on rather than wring his hands in helpless dismay.

Beyond the concentrated insight into Polonius that this action gives, it also suggests an attitude toward him that words cannot exactly delineate. The attitude involves a certain amount of pity and—what is harder to account for objectively—a certain amount of respect. The pity that we feel surfaces when Hamlet says to the dead body, "I took thee for thy better." The sentence makes us realize that Polonius, for all his self-importance, never actually amounted to much, either as a politician or as a man. But somehow in his death Polonius extorts from us a degree of respect. He died because he was trying to be useful, and a close reading of the scene suggests that he may in fact have saved the queen's life at that point—for Hamlet felt a powerful impulse to kill her, and that impulse had been increasing up until Polonius's interruption. Almost by accident, Polonius dies gallantly.

So, now, if we return to Polonius' advice to Laertes, that speech appears to "mean" in two quite different senses. In one way it is a message about affairs in the world, and we can either accept or reject it. In another way, as part of the event-object-meaning which the whole play puts before us, it is also significant. But here the meanings are of a sort that do not find expression in any words but which instead arise out of a combination of circumstances—particular persons dealing with each other, particular actions taking place in particular conditions. We might summarize the difference between these two kinds of meaning in this way: If a person says to us, "I love you," we have a message-meaning; if that same person kisses us, we have an event-object-meaning. We can read literature so as to gain either kind of meaning. Perhaps we should not ignore the message-meanings of literature when they are present. But certainly we lose the most valuable part of great literary works if we search them exclusively for messages. The emotional high-point of Wordsworth's poem "Michael" is the line "And never lifted up a single stone." As message-meaning the line is trivial; as event-object-meaning it has enormous import.

When we try to teach our students to attend to a literary work as an event-object-meaning, we must look for the methods that will help them to experience the work rather than merely to think about it. In the chapter on teaching methods I have suggested some means of presenting works as sensuous things and as happenings, and in the second section of this book, where I offer readings and teaching plans of four works, I attempt to show the use of those means in teaching specific works. I have observed in my own classes that teaching literature as art has at least one advantage: When students ask what the work *is* and what it *does,* the question of what it *means* becomes less awesome and less intractable for them.

Teaching Grows from Reading

There is a second assumption underlying the suggestions in this book. It is that teaching literature ought to grow out of the teacher's and student's reading of it. One can hardly imagine a good teacher who prefers teaching literature to reading it, and probably good teachers who think otherwise simply do not understand that their best teaching is an outgrowth and continuation of their reading, not something apart from it. Typically we decide to teach those works that we like best, hence our desire to teach our specialty. Then, when we teach these works, we present them in a way that opens up our students' minds to just those qualities that we ourselves have discerned. Thus, if we take Golding's *Lord of the Flies* to be a despairing picture of the triumph of savagery over civilization, we emphasize Piggy's murder when we teach it; if we think that the novel allows some chance for civilization, we emphasize Ralph's eventual rescue. Similarly, we present the pig's severed head as a symbol of an achieved fact if we read the book in one way, but as a warning of a dreadful possibility if we read it in another way. Or, finally, if the work strikes us as irresolvably ambiguous, we give equal emphasis to the evidence on both sides of the question.

Since our methods of teaching a work derive to a very large extent from our understanding of that work, a thorough teaching plan obviously must deal with the subject—the particular work and its reception in the reader's consciousness—before it proceeds to methods. For this reason, in the teaching plans offered in the second section of this book, I begin with my own reading of the work that is to be taught. All the works are powerful and rich, and in my short commentaries I do not indicate a full reading of them. But I hope that I have given enough to serve as a basis for suggesting the qualities which the recommended methods should disclose to students.

The relationship between teaching and reading certainly works in both directions, and students enlarge and deepen their teachers' understanding of literature, sometimes by confirming the teachers' insights, sometimes by correcting their insights, and fairly often by giving teachers fresh ideas about works. I tried to remember this complex relationship when I wrote about teaching literature; as a result, the teaching plans include criticism which I omitted from the formal commentaries on the works but which might easily come up in class discussion, and I also have kept the teaching plans at least partly open-ended to allow for original contributions from the students.

Part I

1 Literature as Event

Literature is one of the arts, and reading literature is an artistic, or aesthetic, experience that has something in common with such other aesthetic experiences as listening to music, watching dance, or looking at paintings. Just as a good teacher in one of the other arts will help students to watch or to listen in the best way, so a good teacher of literature, as a first step, will want to show students how to read literature. And since reading literature sharply differs from other kinds of reading, the teacher of literature should decide what the difference is in order to help students to master it. The main purpose of this chapter is to decide what the reading of literature involves. In that connection, we shall look at two questions in particular: What happens to a person who is reading literature successfully? and What capabilities must a reader of literature possess?

We can best begin by making some elementary discriminations of different kinds of mental behavior. The following vignette should help by giving examples of the different kinds of attention which we accord to the objects that we experience in our daily lives. From time to time we shall come back to this vignette for clarification of the distinctions that help to define the aesthetic experience of reading literature.

Imagine the following events. It is a working day—Monday let us suppose—and you have decided to start the week well by getting up early and eating a good breakfast. (1) The alarm goes off at six, and you get up immediately. (2) You prepare yourself a fine breakfast—grapefruit, bacon, eggs, toast, coffee—and you eat it with gusto. (3) After you finish breakfast you have a few minutes to spare, so you look at the morning newspaper. You study the entertainment section because you want to see a movie in the evening. You only glance at the headlines on the front page—so inattentively that you probably could not say what was the chief news story of the day. (4) You get ready for your drive to school. As you start the car you look at your watch; you have the comfortable sensation of being ahead of things even though you do not notice precisely what time it is. As you drive along you stay reasonably alert to signs and to other drivers, but not exceptionally so. For instance, you do not notice that traffic is lighter than usual or that there is a different school crossing guard at an intersection that you always pass. (5) But then something happens that arouses your interest. You drive past a house that is on fire. In a sudden, frightening glimpse as your car passes, you see the fire trucks with their flashing lights, a police car or two, much smoke, and the hoses pouring water. A crowd has gathered and watches with interest, but the fire makes you so uneasy that you are glad to drive on and get out of the neighborhood. (6) Soon after, another episode occurs that strikes you in a very different way. As you stop for a traffic signal that has just turned red, you notice on the corner to your right an extremely pretty girl who runs across the street in front of you and throws herself into the arms of a handsome young man who waits for her on the opposite corner. They kiss and walk down the street hand in hand. Pleased, you watch them in the rear-view mirror until the car behind you honks, you realize that the traffic light has turned green, and you drive on to school to begin the day's teaching.

This early-morning episode presents a variety of experiences which we can differentiate from one another by using opposite terms. First, we can divide the experiences into those that are conscious and those that are unconscious or nearly so. For instance, you were unconscious or barely conscious of all the items in the newspaper except the entertainment columns, of the new crossing guard, and of the exact state of the traffic. In addition, you were only sort of half-conscious of the time. (Most people, indeed, look at their watches but are then unable to say what time it is because they merely looked to see where the hands pointed, reassuring themselves that they were on schedule.) Many other facts not mentioned in the vignette also escaped you. Almost certainly you did not notice your breathing or the beating of your heart or any number of other purely physiological actions (we notice such things only when we are in an abnormal condition). And details of the weather such as the kind of clouds in the sky and the degree of humidity, probably escaped you altogether.

In the story of your Monday morning, however, there were a number of events which your consciousness fully enveloped—the taste of breakfast, the entertainment announcements in the newspaper, the fire, the young lovers. In respect to our consciousness of the world around us we resemble an enormous battleship under bombardment: The ship is impervious to bullets, and shells and rockets merely disturb it; only the torpedoes and bombs affect it. We too are bombarded with countless stimuli, but only certain ones thoroughly touch consciousness. In an important way we are unlike the ship, however—it cannot change its environment by wishing it away; it must endure the bombardment. We, on the other hand, can to a greater or lesser degree decide which stimuli we will notice and which we will ignore. Attention can be trained to grip some features of the surroundings but to turn away from others.

Having distinguished between conscious and unconscious experiences, we can now focus on the conscious experiences in the Monday-morning story and make some distinctions about them. An obvious difference is that some of them were pleasant and some unpleasant. For me at least, the pleasant experiences would have been eating breakfast, scanning the paper, knowing that I was on schedule, and, most of all, seeing the young lovers, and the unpleasant experiences would have included waking up to an alarm and seeing a house on fire.

Before making a further distinction among the pleasant experiences, we should consider the fact that the same event will give pleasure to one person and pain to another. This fact bears heavily on the teaching of literature and, for that matter, all the other arts as well. I have indicated two experiences in the story which for me are always unpleasant—being awakened by an alarm clock and seeing a house on fire—and yet I know that many others enjoy these experiences. I have friends who, like Browning's Pippa, have a positive lust to get out of bed in the morning, who imagine that an hour spent sleeping is an hour wasted. As for fires, though I get away from them as soon as I can, I notice that they always draw a crowd of intent onlookers. But preference also works in the opposite direction: things that are pleasant to me sometimes displease and even disgust others. For example, eating breakfast and seeing lovers meet and embrace are experiences that I like but which some others do not. Some people are so fastidious about food that they eat only for nourishment, and many more people have developed a habit of starting the day with only a light breakfast or none at all. As for the lovers (whom I like more than any of the other events in the story), some people would condemn them as exhibitionists (and me as a voyeur).

This difference in taste—the predilection of different people for different and sometimes even opposite things—extends to the arts as well as to other fields. The same person may even find a certain thing unpleasant at one time but pleasant at another. The great conductor Bruno Walter, in a recorded interview with Arnold Michaelis,[1] confessed that when he was a young music director near the beginning of his long career he had reservations about the symphonies of Bruckner. He thought they were prolix, relentlessly churning through the same material with very little variation. But Walter suffered a severe illness, and from then on his view of Bruckner changed. What Walter had sensed before as mere loquacity, in his new frame of mind came to appear as weight and substance.

Walter's experience underlines some points that should be considered in connection with artistic taste. One is that taste in a serious art lover is not the same as whim; it expresses a deep bias of personality and viewpoint. Thus, Walter's earlier doubt about Bruckner was based on a just admiration of that concision in art which Bruckner does really lack, though he offsets this defect by great merits of another kind. Even more worth noting in Walter's account of his response to Bruckner is the point that the tastes of people who love art do not merely change, they grow. The vicissitudes of Walter's life had corrected his earlier, more callow opinion by giving him wisdom, a fuller sense of the preciousness of life, and of realities beyond the temporal self.

Now, to continue the series of distinctions among our Monday-morning experiences: With respect to the pleasant occurrences we can distinguish between the experiences that are satisfying and those that are gratifying. The difference has to do with a person's needs; experiences that are satisfying fulfill evident needs, and those that are gratifying are pleasant even though they answer no conscious need. Thus, in the story the breakfast was satisfying because it assuaged the need for food; the morning newspaper satisfied the palpable need to arrange the evening schedule; the watch satisfied the need to be on time. Another way of making the same point would be to say that a satisfying experience is a means to some end beyond itself: eating is a means of getting nourishment, reading newspapers a means of acquiring information, looking at watches a means of knowing the time. On the other hand, watching the young lovers was a gratifying experience; it was not a means, it was an end, simply a pleasure in itself. The fire, too, was pleasing or gratifying for those who enjoyed watching it, but it fulfilled no need.

A further point about gratifying experiences which ought to be made is that things can be valuable without at the same time being useful. Gratifying experiences, like seeing the young lovers or listening to symphonies or reading novels, are not events that strictly fulfill a need in the direct way that learning to multiply or to spell does. This difference can cause apprehension in a teacher of literature. There are a number of good answers to give a student who asks why it is necessary to learn to spell, but there is less certainty of what to say to one who asks why it is necessary to read literature, particularly if that student has not yet learned to like it. Compared with such obviously needed abilities as spelling or correct usage or composition, reading literature may seem to be merely the self-indulgence of lotus-eaters who would rather fornicate with the muse than do useful work. The teacher who is in that mood should be reminded that not all valuable things are useful, and not all useful things are valuable. Lying, which would never be committed if it did not satisfy needs, is certainly more useful than honesty, which more often than not frustrates the satisfaction of need. But honesty is valuable just the same. So are the arts.

These experiences also distinguish between the arrest and nonarrest of attention. Experiences in which attention is sharply and suddenly aroused are those set off by the lovers, the fire, and the alarm clock. All these experiences have a knock-your-eye (or ear)-out quality that is felt with a degree of shock. The alarm clock abruptly shocks us out of our sleep. The fire shocks us out of our quiescence. The lovers also affect us in a way akin to shock, seeming to put us suddenly into a new and different state, but in this experience the shock happens to be pleasant, so we are likely to give it a pleasant name—*charm,* perhaps, or *interest.* By contrast, eating breakfast and scanning the newspaper do not arrest attention. Perhaps they would have done so had they been raised to a higher level of intensity—had the breakfast, for example, changed from plain bacon and eggs to an omelette of Julia Child perfection, or had the newspaper become an essay by Virginia Woolf. But those transformations would have made the experiences something other than mere breakfast or just the newspaper.

Events not only can arrest attention, stop it for a moment; they can fix or prolong attention so that it comes to rest on a particular thing instead of flickering on to other objects. This fact leads to another distinction, that between the fixation and nonfixation of attention. Looking over the Monday-morning activities, we see that one of them fixed attention and all the others dissipated it. It was the lovers, of course, who fixed our attention. We could not get enough of them and we watched them with a steady interest, so oblivious of everything else that we were unaware of the change in the traffic light until the car behind sounded its horn. The sight of those lovers fully absorbed all our attention, so that in our minds the little episode completely stood out by itself. Eating breakfast and scanning the newspaper, on the other hand, did not fix attention in anything like the same degree. These two events naturally flowed into adjacent activities. For instance, we could easily have breakfasted and glanced through the paper at the same time, whereas the sight of the lovers made us forget about watching the traffic signal. The alarm clock illustrates the difference between arresting attention and fixing it. Although it shocked us from sleep, it did not sustain interest; in fact, the instinctive response was to turn off the alarm as soon as possible.

The various experiences that we passed through also differed in respect to their power to direct our attention. The distinction is between controlling and noncontrolling experiences. The breakfast and the drive (except the encounter with the lovers) were noncontrolling experiences; they failed to fill and shape our minds in the way that air fills a balloon or, better, the way that the current of a river is shaped by all the fluctuations in the bank and the river bed. As we ate breakfast and, still more, as we drove along the street, our minds were free to think about other things than eating or driving. We could very well have planned one of the day's classes as we ate, for example, or enjoyed a Walter Mittyish fantasy as we drove. On the other hand, reading the entertainment section in the newspaper exercised a good deal of control over our attention. We studied the columns of illustrated notices, getting a clear conception of the theater, the film, and the times in each case, our minds successively resting on each one. Still more obviously controlling our attention were the lovers. It was not merely that they excluded all else from our minds; they formed our consciousness (*informed* in the original sense, gave consciousness a form by entering into and filling it), at least for a few moments. Interest was aroused when the pretty girl flitted across the street in front of us, and it intensified in a burst of pleasure when we saw her and the young man embracing; then came the more quiet resolution of the episode as they walked away hand in hand. A common saying is that a particular event made us "all eyes." Psychologically it would be more accurate to say that we became "all event." At any rate, certain happenings do that for us; they absorb our personalities for a time, shaping them independently of our own thinking and willing. In extreme instances of this sort we may say that we have just been in a brown study, or had a daydream, a trance, or a vision.

A final difference among these experiences is their resolution or irresolution. Only one of the episodes induces absolute closure, really wraps itself up into a unit that is separate from everything else. That, of course, is the episode of the lovers. When they drift from our vision as we drive on, we feel that it is all completely right and, even though we shall rehearse the genial scene many times in our memory, it also is all over. Nothing needs to be done with the lovers, and nothing has to be done because of them. They stand apart all by themselves. We have to do something with the alarm or because of it (turn it off and get up), with the breakfast (digest it and wash the dishes), and with all the other events. But the lovers exist apart from the flux of affairs that keep shifting and changing and always demanding that we do something.

Now that we have reviewed the Monday-morning occurrences, we see that one, the sight of the lovers, stands out as being different from all the others. That episode had a mixture of characteristics which none of the others possessed. It was pleasant (as the alarm was not). It pleased without answering to some felt need (unlike the breakfast, the newspaper, or the watch). It arrested our attention (as the newspaper did not). It fixed attention (unlike the fire). It controlled attention (unlike breakfast). Finally, of all these experiences, the episode of the lovers was the one that concluded attention, that completed itself so that we had nothing to do to it or because of it.

The sight provided us an aesthetic experience. It belonged to the very large realm of things that we call, collectively, the beautiful, and that includes, on one side, such formal, arranged experiences as looking at paintings, listening to music, watching dance, and reading literature and, on another side, the more spontaneous and less predictable events of watching a tennis match, listening to a thunderstorm, or examining snowflakes on a windowpane. The episode of the lovers possessed certain characteristics that associated it with other aesthetic experiences and set it off from experiences that were not aesthetic.

A feature which all aesthetic experiences have in common is that they are pleasant. Moreover, they are pleasant in a special way; they exist because of the abundance of life, not the necessities, and they make us happy even though they fulfill no urgent personal need. Another characteristic of aesthetic experience is the way in which they dominate our attention, a domination that includes arrest, fixation, control, and resolution. Since reading literature is one form of aesthetic experience, it has all these same characteristics. To expand on this point, the person who reads literature successfully will have a highly conscious and thoroughly pleasant experience, independent of any personal need, in which the particular work that is being read arrests the reader's attention, fixes it, controls it, and concludes it. In recent years, writers on the teaching of literature have generally referred to this complex process by a sort of verbal shorthand, calling it *engagement*. In later chapters, when we look for means of teaching works, we often deal with the problem of helping students to engage with literature.

At present, however, we shall ignore that special question and point instead to certain more general consequences for teachers regarding the conclusions about aesthetic experience which we have just reached. One consequence is that aesthetic experience is by no means limited to literature; it also embraces all the other high arts and, with somewhat diminished intensity and in modified form, the popular arts and certain aspects of sport, nature study, animal life, and social life. Indeed, it can crop up almost anywhere. A second consequence of our description is that aesthetic experience must be widespread and not at all an elitist entertainment. Although the aesthetic experience is difficult to describe accurately, it seems not to be a difficult experience to entertain. Most people appear to have these experiences in one form or another, although it may not be a form that English teachers heartily recommend. Once I sat at a bar next to a man who avidly watched a football game on the television set. One of the players made a long touchdown run, and my neighbor, beside himself with joy, shouted, "He's beautiful! He's beautiful!" Probably that man would rather die than say the same thing of a fine dancer like Nureyev or Bujones, but the fact remains that the man loved the beautiful as well as he could. We all love it, blinded though we are to some of its multitudinous dimensions. The people who really prefer ugliness to beauty—who deliberately cultivate an ungainly posture, for instance, or choose repulsive clothing—must be as rare as those who prefer death to life.

If we are inclined to think that our students do not really love the beautiful, the main reason for our pessimism is likely to be our observation that many of them do not care for beauty in the forms prescribed by the school curriculum or by ourselves. But a love of Shakespeare's sonnets or Mozart's symphonies is a product of high culture that is gradually engendered in a totally nourishing spiritual environment. People who come to enjoy these things do so bit by bit, through stages of growing acuity. At any level of their development, however, people have some kinds of aesthetic experiences that they cherish. If they do not seek the beautiful in classic art forms such as literature and dance, they may find it in the outdoors, and if not there, then perhaps in sport on its aesthetic side or in the little lives of their pets, very poignant and luminous of value for those who have eyes to see. In short, a real case of aesthetic blankness is probably as rare as paralysis or amnesia.

Well then, one might object, if the appetite for beautiful things is common, there can hardly be any need for teaching literature. Why not just put books in our students' hands and let them be guided by their lusty craving for the beautiful? Or, if it happens that they make no headway in literature, why not let them devote themselves to some of the other high arts or to popular art or nature? These are important questions for at least two reasons. One is that in their more sinister embodiments (like "Why teach Milton to students who are satisfied with Mary Worth?"), such questions can be very demoralizing to an English teacher. Another is that even though the questions misrepresent the real case, still they can help us get to some points about teaching literature that we might otherwise miss.

Why Teach Literature?

As for the first question, why teach literature if people generally love the beautiful, the answer grows out of the distinction between appetite and aptitude. We have many forceful drives, or appetites, but we simply do not know how to fulfill some of them until we are taught, and carefully taught at that. Teachers, of all people, should have examples of this fact. Most of us have known students who eagerly desired to be liked and "to get along with people" but did not know how to go about it. They had to be taught, counseled, in other words. Driving a car or playing cards or pleasing the other sex are the same; we all want to do these things, but we cannot succeed in them without being taught. We can add the reading of literature to the list of agreeable skills that must be taught in order to be exercised.

The notion that appreciation of such a beautiful thing as literature need not be taught because everyone naturally loves the beautiful therefore is untrue. Nevertheless it is neighbor to a truth that English teachers must recognize if they are to do their work well. If the love of beauty really is a natural feeling, then the teacher's main task, after giving what help is indispensable, is to get out of the way of the student's appreciation. Even though the teacher knows interesting facts about the author which the student does not know, or has true insights into the work which the student has not yet discerned, still there comes a time when the teacher must practice restraint. That time is the moment when the student begins, independently, to appreciate, to perceive the work as it is, to make vital connections between the work and the self or between the work and the rest of the world. The restraint is not easy, particularly for a teacher who imagines that the only thing to be done with a literary work is to talk about it. But the time comes when we must stop analyzing it lest we talk it to death, and distract students with information about the work when they are ready for the real thing itself. In this regard teachers can learn from the birds, who do not lecture their young about aviation when they are ready to fly, but sweetly expel them from the nest instead.

All artistic apprehension involves some degree of adventuring, of working through problems oneself and finding one's own solutions. We are more disposed to talk about a work *after* we have begun to assimilate it than before. The teacher, who has already made the discoveries, must not be in such a hurry to communicate them that the student has no chance for self-exploration and discovery. If literature were nothing more than the microbes that might be described in a biology lecture, there would be no objection to extended discussion of it, for we can learn about objects through informed talk. But art objects involve us in a much fuller and more complex experience than do other objects; our transactions with them are very rich. They are objects, to be sure, but they are also events, interior happenings. To the extent that they are objects we can talk about them just as biologists can talk about microbes, but when they become events, talk must cease for a while so that we can attend to what is happening to us as we read or see or listen.

Why Not Alternatives to Literature?

The other question is why not let the students who show little progress in literary study pursue one of the other art forms or popular culture or nature study instead? This question is harder to deal with, and an entirely truthful answer may not altogether please us. To begin, one notices that the alternatives offered to literature are very broad, including all the classic art forms plus film, television, popular music, outdoor appreciation, animal study, and sport. We had better divide the list into two parts—into the traditional art forms on the one hand and all the other aesthetic products on the other—and then find an answer to the original question with respect to each part.

First, why not encourage students who are backward in appreciating literature to take up one of the other arts? Well, appreciation of these arts also needs to be learned, and unfortunately literature is the only art form that is taught in schools for anything like an adult level of appreciation. Of dance and architecture there is nothing but an occasional assembly program. Art and music, rarely taught for appreciation, are more widely available as performance studies. But even if we make the risky assumption that performance leads to appreciation, the outlook for art and music is not good. A high school student who is lucky will get a year, perhaps two or three, of an art course that, sprawling all over a huge field, offers slight instruction in clay sculpting, water coloring, working in oils, figure drawing, lettering, stenciling, and so on. At the end of the course it is a fortunate student who knows the difference between a lithograph and a palette. The case with music is a little different. Some—comparatively few—school systems produce musicians who can play beautifully by the time they have reached their high school years. But in most schools the student musician is more likely to spend eight or ten years on the xylophone or marimba, celebrating his accomplishment and punishing his audience at football matches and PTA meetings by thumping his way through *In a Persian Market* and various Sousa marches. There may be valuable learning in such a curriculum; certainly stoic fortitude has a chance to flourish. But such learning as there may be is not connected with art, either with its production or its appreciation.

The conclusion to be reached from all this is that, in most high schools, literature is the only art form that is taught for appreciation at a high level. Art and music are taught mainly for performance, and the remaining arts are scarcely taught at all. Perhaps school curriculums will eventually embrace a broader range of aesthetic education than they do now, but for the present, in most schools, the student's range of aesthetic choice is between literature and nothing at all.

This lack of a full spectrum of art appreciation for students is the reason why the English teacher can confidently emphasize literature as, for practical purposes, the most available art form for study. But it also suggests an added set of duties for the English teacher. Until the good time comes when aesthetic education assumes something like equal importance with scientific and humanistic education, someone must try to fill the gap. The English teacher is one of the better qualified persons to do it. Although perhaps not *well* qualified, the English teacher can at least make students conscious of the variety and interest that all the different forms of art can hold for their lives. Students can be told of coming dance performances, of noteworthy television programs, and plays and concerts. Films that the teacher has seen can be discussed, preferably while those films are still showing in local theaters.

The English teacher also can help students greatly by telling them of the simple facts, perfectly familiar to the teacher but mysteries to many young people, that surround the arts and unfortunately help to barricade them. At least some high school students will need to know the answers to such questions as these: How many performers are in a quartet? If you do not enjoy a performance, is there a time when it is polite to leave? Do you have to pay admission to get into an art museum, or do you have to be a member? Are you supposed to buy something before you leave an art show? Can you wear jeans to museums and concert halls? How do you know when to applaud at a concert so that you do not interrupt the music and make a fool of yourself? The simplicity of these questions may be surprising but the teacher will take them seriously just the same, for the ignorance they express can be a powerful obstacle to young persons who are trying to approach art, and it is an obstacle that can be removed for them just as it was once removed for the teacher.

We have dealt with the first half of the aesthetic alternatives to literature —the other classic arts—and have concluded that although English teachers should do what they can to make those arts available, still the primacy belongs to literature. For a somewhwat related reason the other opportunities for aesthetic experience must be neglected in the English classroom just as they unfortunately are largely ignored elsewhere in the school. The reason is that English teachers lack expertise in these fields. Cautious attempts have been made from time to time to include popular arts in the English curriculum. A generation ago, high school English classes made room for a unit on radio, which later was supplanted by the television unit, and for many years some English teachers have tried to introduce poetry through popular songs. Little has been done on a broad scale, however, and this comparative neglect seems inevitable. To justify it, one need not argue that the popular arts have less quality than the fine arts; it is sufficient to point out that they have a very different *kind* of quality. There are many interesting comic strips, for example, but the characteristics that make them interesting are neither literary nor pictorial. We admire *Blondie* neither for its plotting nor for its figure drawing. This difference in kind of quality also holds true with music; *Over the Rainbow* delights everyone, but the delight that it gives is altogether different from the delight provided by an art song quite like it in theme, the Wolf-Goethe *Kennst Du Das Land?* In short, the English teacher has an even more distant relation to the popular arts than to the classic arts other than literature. English teachers, like everyone else, are somewhat familiar with popular arts, but essentially these arts are even farther off their professional map than the classic arts because they possess a different kind of quality and are a different sort of thing. Some might argue that English teachers ought to develop a professional competence in teaching the popular arts, but a persuasive answer is that they have enough to do already. As with the classic arts other than literature, it may be that the proper teaching of popular art will have to wait until curriculum makers recognize the rightful place and scope of aesthetic education. Meanwhile most English teachers will treat this field sympathetically but sparingly.

There remain the other principal aesthetic alternatives to literature: experience with the outdoors, animals, and sport. Here, too, most English teachers are at a loss. Even though they themselves may participate in one or another of these experiences, they have not made a professional study of them. And, again, they can hardly be asked to.

2 Literature as Object

It is a fact proved by common observation that if you hold a cat before a mirror the cat will not see itself; neither will it see you. Similarly, we can tell that when a cat looks at a picture of a cat on the wall or on the television screen, it sees a blob of light, certainly, but nothing that it discerns as a cat. Whether it is the cat who is wrong in this matter or ourselves, whether that object in the looking-glass is reality, illusion, or delusion, are questions which we shall have to leave to the epistemologists. Nonetheless, this observation that the cat sees nothing in the mirror but untranslated bits of light is in a certain way very familiar to us. In our teaching of literature we often see a human behavior that is closely analogous to the cat's: The novice reader looks into the pages of a book, and sees, hears, and feels nothing but the pages of that book—flickering, perhaps, with words that are recognized but which no more turn into sights and sounds, persons and feelings, than the blobs of light on the television screen become an object for the cat who watches. But fortunately for our success as teachers, the analogy between the cat who sees nothing but lights in the mirror and the reader who sees nothing but words on the page soon breaks down; for although the cat will never learn to see cats in mirrors, the novice reader can learn to see more than words on a page. The purpose of this chapter is to examine that function of transmuting words into things. I shall call this function *constituting* or *constitution*.[1]

What constituting amounts to can best be shown by giving some examples of the process first, and later offering a general analysis. An exceptionally clear example of constituting occurs in *Macbeth,* Act I, Scene 7. That is the scene in which Lady Macbeth has to stir up the hesitating Macbeth to go ahead with his plan to murder Duncan. Macbeth never gets to finish his sentence that begins, "If we should fail," for Lady Macbeth suddenly interrupts him with these words:

> We fail!
> But screw your courage to the sticking-place,
> And we'll not fail.

(I, vii, 59–61)

And then she goes on to detail her plan for murdering Duncan, the plan which in fact they put into operation and which succeeds.

We can read those lines just quoted in two basically different ways, and those different ways of reading will produce two very different images of Lady Macbeth. One reading can be expressed in this paraphrase: "If we do fail, then we simply have to take the consequences that inevitably follow. However, if you act resolutely now, our chances of failure are diminished." Read in this way, the lines would get a stress pattern like this:

We FAIL!

But . . . screw your courage to the sticking-place,
And we'll NOT fail.

Another reading goes like this: "We certainly shall not fail if you will only behave as you should." This second reading gives the following stress pattern:

WE . . . FAIL

But screw your courage to the sticking-place,
AND WE'LL NOT FAIL.

On the first reading Lady Macbeth is a quasi-fatalist who both thinks that our fates are determined by necessities outside ourselves, and at the same time illogically believes that we may be able to influence our fortunes by vigorous action. On the second reading she is a violent woman obsessed with the certainty that she and Macbeth, fully controlling their own lives, can take whatever they want. Actually these two different readings can be blended together into a third possibility, which happens to be the reading that I find most congenial. It is that Lady Macbeth really feels fatalistic about the murder but she pretends to be confident in order to strengthen Macbeth's resolution.

In any case, whichever of these readings we take, the two basic ones or the combination, certain points can be made about what we are doing. One of these points is that we are not yet at the level of interpreting the work. *Macbeth* does not even exist as an object of contemplation, a drama that can be interpreted, until we have made for ourselves an image of Lady Macbeth. Therefore, this decision about the reading of her speech on the possibility of failure belongs to a more basic level than interpretation, a level at which we are making, or constituting, the object to which at later stages we shall react in various ways. A second point about these readings is that none of them is, properly speaking, based on literary "evidence." Punctuation in this case does not help at all, for although a modern writer could mechanically distinguish between the two basic readings ("We fail." versus "We! Fail?"), even he could not indicate the combination, and as for Shakespeare, Elizabethan typography and punctuation were so irregular that they can give us no hint of his intended reading. Nor does context furnish a clue here, for everything in the play that argues for one of the readings can just as easily be made to support another. For instance, the helpless apathy of Lady Macbeth in the sleepwalking scene can support the fatalistic reading, on the ground that she had in her from the beginning a depression which later deepened into a catatonic withdrawal. On the other hand, we can take the same bit of context as a sign that her sufferings have radically altered her basic character. Either argument from context is equally good and does not settle for us what reading we shall take.

What, then, is the basis on which we take one reading or another? In this case the answer seems to be that we rely on an estimate of likelihood that comes from within ourselves, not from the play. We choose the reading which gives us the character that we can most readily imagine. We are basing our judgment on bits of "evidence," which are more private and personal to ourselves than they are demonstrable aspects of the text. The reading that I have just confessed to prefer no doubt tells as much about my image of women as it tells about Shakespeare's, but I think that I need not be embarrassed about that, for the same thing can be said about any other reader of *Macbeth*. In some measure all of us make up the play as we read it. We have to, in order for it to exist as a literary work at all.

Keats's "Ode to a Nightingale" provides numerous instances of constituting. One of them occurs in the second stanza, where Keats expresses his yearning to drink wine.

> O for a beaker full of the warm South,
> Full of the true, the blushful Hippocrene,
> With beaded bubbles winking at the brim,
> And purple-stained mouth.

The last two lines give the instance of constituting here. Just as with Lady Macbeth's speech, alternative readings are possible. One reading that the lines will impart consists of two objects, the glass which has wine bubbles glittering about the rim and, near to it, a human mouth stained by the wine. That image, in a crude representation, would look like this:

But the lines equally well support a different picture. As we look at the full goblet of wine, first the glistening bubbles at the top become two eyes, one winking at us, and then we add a mouth to the glass so as to transform it into a bright-eyed, waggish Silenus inviting us to drink and be merry. That picture would look like this:

Again, as with Lady Macbeth's speech, no evidence exists to tell us which of the two different readings to take. The context supports either of the constructions as well as the other, and no remarks by Keats on these lines are recorded. Here, too, therefore, we do our constituting independently of the text, but in this case the basis will probably not be the same as it is with Lady Macbeth. With her we choose one reading over the other in accordance with our idea of how she would behave in that situation; verisimilitude seems to be the test. The basis for selecting a particular constituting of Keats's lines seems to be satisfaction; we probably select the reading that most pleases us. My own choice is the second of the two.

One well-known example of constituting in fiction is Frank Stockton's "Lady and the Tiger," in which the text of the story will not tell the reader whether it was a beautiful lady who entered into the Coliseum to be the hero's wife, or a tiger to kill him.[2] A similar example, on a higher level, is Henry James's *Turn of the Screw*. In reading that novella we must decide for ourselves whether the governess was psychotic (and the story is a study in deviant psychology) or whether she was sane (and the story is a ghost tale). Probably most interpretations that have a long history of critical controversy —like interpretations of Keats's great odes—are constitutings of the work in question which rely for evidence on critics' sensibilities rather than on palpable aspects of the work. The dispute concerning Hamlet's delay seems to be another case of a scholarly quarrel over a literary constituting. Was Hamlet a man incapacitated for action by an excess of thoughtfulness, or was he an effective doer who acted as soon as he reasonably could? The play itself does not clearly answer that question; hence the controversy grows out of different constitutings.

Intelligence before Interpretation

Now that we have examined some instances of constituting, we should be able to generalize upon the process. Underlying the idea of constituting is the conception of the work of art as being in itself porous like a sponge rather than hard and resistant like a diamond. The art work—the poem or story—is formed so that it can receive and accommodate intelligence in much the same way that the sponge can take in water and retain it. If we want to mystify ourselves about the nature of sponges, we can ask if they are more or less themselves when they contain water or when they are dry. But if we tried the same question with literature and other art works and asked if they are more or less themselves by being constituted with the audience's informing intelligence, we should find that at this level the comparison between sponges and art works breaks down. Wet or dry, sponges are whatever they are. Not so art works; they are nothing but gibbering ghosts of themselves until they have been constituted by a receiving intelligence. Emerson had such an idea as this in mind when he remarked that "one must be an inventor to read well."[3]

Constituting needs to be distinguished from interpreting. Constituting occurs first, and it answers the question, "What *is* this work?" It takes a mere text and turns it into a poem. It belongs, therefore, to the level of perception, even though the object that is perceived has some of the viewer's qualities of life envisagement projected onto it. Once the poem has been constituted, the process of interpretation can begin, and the question can be asked, "What does this poem mean?" As a matter of fact, constituting is even an early stage in perception, and much of what we perceive in a poem requires that we constitute it first. Thus, although we can see that Poe's "To Helen" is a sonnet without troubling to constitute it, we cannot even perceive that the poem is mysterious rather than bright and distinct unless we first constitute it by filling it out with our own sensibility. To sum up, it is the work *as constituted* (after we have filled it out and filled it in) that we describe as "the poem" or "the story." We constitute a work before we interpret it, and our feelings and thoughts about it are later stages of reaction.

It is in the constituting of a work that the personal and the private play a large part. Different readers will constitute works in accordance with their own different sensibilities—sensibilities that include not only so-called identity themes of personality but also memories, moral convictions, formal learning in many subjects, and all sorts of experiences. Furthermore, constituting is a continuous process. We can substitute a different constituting for one we accepted earlier, or we can add constitutings to each other. My own reading experience with two of the examples just given illustrates both substitution and addition. For years I read the lines from Keats's Nightingale Ode as describing two different objects, a glass and human lips near it, and the other constituting of those lines never occurred to me until I found it in some critic's commentary. The reading of Lady Macbeth's speech for which I have stated my preference—the one that combines the two basic and divergent constitutings—first suggested itself to me when I wrote this chapter. We not only substitute one constituting for another or combine them, we also actually take opposite ones sometimes and accept them all, though not in the same reading perhaps. Kafka's *The Trial* is an example. That novel can be taken as an expression of man's alienation from God, or as a description of the interaction of the id, ego, and superego, or as an account of life in a tuberculosis sanitarium. Critics have given persuasive arguments for all three readings,[4] and at various times I have constituted the work with pleasure each way.

When we speak of a work's "richness" we are probably referring mainly to its susceptibility to a variety of constitutings. Some constitutings we reject, some we accept, others we combine; then as we live with a work and grow with it, we accept readings that we previously rejected, and in another stage we take readings which contradict each other and accept now one, now another. Our lives pour into the work, and in our successive readings of it we find the benchmarks of our spiritual biographies.

In *Autocrat of the Breakfast-Table,* Oliver Wendell Holmes succinctly expresses the private dimension in reading literature and at the same time shows the enriching effect that this private dimension exerts on our apprehension.

> Now I tell you a poem must be kept *and used,* like a meerschaum, or a violin. A poem is just as porous as the meerschaum; the more porous it is, the better. I mean to say that a genuine poem is capable of absorbing an indefinite amount of the essences of our humanity,—its tenderness, its heroism, its regrets, its aspiration, so as to be gradually stained through with a divine secondary color derived from ourselves. So you see it must take time to bring the sentiment of the poem into harmony with our nature, by staining ourselves through every thought and image our being can penetrate.[5]

The constituted work, then, necessarily involves a large contribution from the reader. And no two readers are quite the same. If we put these two facts together, do we have to conclude that there is no such thing as a right or normal constituting of any particular work? This question is very important. Indeed, whatever answer the teacher gives to it becomes the basis of the teacher's approach both to his or her own way of reading literature and to the methods of teaching it. If the answer to the question is "no," then the teacher will not try to impose any standard or definitive reading in dealing with a text, and, if this conviction is consistently followed, will try not to prescribe to students any thoughts or feelings—even the teacher's own— that should accompany a given work. In fact, the word *should,* from this point of view, does not apply at all. On this basis the standard of good reading is suggested by words such as *genuine, honest, sincere, spontaneous, original.* If, on the other hand, the teacher believes the right, normal readings are possible, the question of why serious readers do disagree on some points regarding literary works must be asked, and the argument that the fact of such disagreement shows that normal readings cannot exist must also be dealt with. Furthermore, in planning lessons, the teacher will seek methods that lead students to discover normal readings on their own, not just obediently to recite some authority's views.

What arguments can be adduced that favor the subjectivist approach, and what arguments exist against it?[6] The main favorable argument has already been examined, but to summarize it now, we can say that whenever a literary work comes into actual, real, full existence it does so in the sensibility of the particular person who reads it, and that it necessarily takes on the coloring of that person's temperament, age, disposition, and other qualities. That is not an "ought" statement, a statement about the way people ought to read literature; it is an "is" statement, a statement about the way they do read it. It is not a matter of choice. If you or I or our students read *Oedipus* (or look at *Guernica* or listen to the *Eroica*), we inevitably do so with *our* brains and *our* hearts, not Aristotle's or Matthew Arnold's. That much seems certain.

But there are also arguments that work against the view that any reader's constituting is as good as any other reader's. One of these arguments stems from the obvious fact that we keep changing our minds about particular works. We keep reevaluating them for their beauty, their importance, their meaning; we sometimes shift our constitutings of given passages. Ultimately, I think, these variations in our readings have to be explained in one of two ways. One explanation is to claim that our characters keep changing so much, as we come back to the same work at different times, because we are not really the same persons we were when we read it previously. The other explanation, and the more reasonable one, is that we change our successive constitutings of a work because, in spite of whatever indefiniteness and incompleteness the work may have as mere text, nonetheless there exists something basically "there" that we apprehend more or less accurately in our different readings, something that we recognize on one reading, ignore on another. So that if our readings of a work give evidence about ourselves, they also tell us something about the work.

This argument gets support from an easily verifiable fact about literary apprehension. It is the fact of the *inter*subjective. Granted that our thoughts and feelings about a work have got to be our own and not those of someone else that have been imposed upon us, is not the amount of agreement that is to be found among any group of readers very striking? Take Lady Macbeth's lines, for instance. We might disagree on the question of whether they signify a woman who thinks that she and her husband are fated to a predetermined end, or one who thinks they can achieve any ambition of theirs through vigorous will, or one who really thinks the first but pretends to think the second. But certainly we should all agree that Lady Macbeth is intense, high strung, and exhortative in these lines. We can go on to a finer discrimination: Even though Lady Macbeth's passion has temporarily led her into a quarrel with her husband, still we know that she really respects him and never thinks of herself as a domineering wife. And as for Keats's lines, whichever constituting we prefer, we are probably unanimous in agreeing that even though their expression takes the form of happy, carefree bibulousness, their total suggestion is serious and even somber.

This answer can help us to deal with divergent responses, both as readers and as teachers. When two readers discover that their responses to a work differ from each other—in the interpretation of meaning, say, or the visualization of an image—the most likely reason for the difference is not that they are two people so unlike each other as never to see the same thing in the same way. Rather, the story or poem they are examining offers so many possibilities of response that Reader A follows out one possibility, Reader B another. Looking at the situation from the outside, one sees that any one of three combinations is possible: (1) both readers can be wrong, can misconstrue the work; (2) one of them can be right and the other wrong; (3) both can be right and yet differ from each other, as in the case of ambiguities of reference or layers of interpretation. In each of these three combinations, open-minded discussion of the work will help to foster a good reading. If in their different ways both readers are wrong but nevertheless see the other person's mistake, each may be able to reject his own errors. If one offers a correct reading and the other a faulty one, they will be able to see which reading really does fit the work and which one does not. If both have made a response that is accurate but incomplete or perhaps less satisfying than some other response that is also right, they can identify the different possibilities and then select that which is right for them, or even blend the various responses into a fuller reading than either one had at the outset.

The question of whether there exists such a thing as a right or normal reading of a text is so complex that a really careful and accurate answer has to be both "yes" and "no." On the one hand, it is certainly true that reading literature is a subjective experience which derives some of its character from the person who does the reading. Without that there can be none of the vibrancy of excited interest that partly characterizes any aesthetic experience. On the other hand, reading literature also involves the true seeing of an object, something apart from ourselves. Without that, all the wonderfulness and clarity of the experience are lost. So, then, since reading literature requires both a subject (the reader) and an object (the work), it is partly subjective—conditioned by the reader's tastes, sympathies, interests—and it is also partly objective—determined by the work's form. That mixed nature of literary experience, the combination of the subjective and the objective, is exactly the justification for literary criticism and also for less formal discussion of literary works. By learning what others think about a literary work we can acquire a broad range of possible responses, and then out of that range we can select the ones that best suit ourselves without mutilating the work. F. R. Leavis and John Middleton Murry have very different opinions about Fielding. Leavis thinks that Fielding, lacking moral seriousness, does not enter the first rank of English novelists; Murry believes that Fielding was a morally complete man who created characters and situations that fully delineate the nature of love.[7] This is an interesting controversy, interesting because it gives us the responses of two first-rate readers, out of which we can augment or correct or test our own reaction to Fielding.

Our first approach to literary experience was to see it as a dichotomy; the work, or object, was on the one side and the reader, or subject, was on the other. But then, in dealing with the question of which of these two predominated over the other, we produced a three-sided solution; we had the work and the reader, as before, but we added the larger audience of readers, all the discussion which that audience generates, and the intersubjective response which that audience generates, and the intersubjective response which it authenticates. Our instinct as teachers will make us welcome this solution, for we like discussion, knowing that it is a useful means to provoke interest and even to impart understanding. We need to be on our guard, however. Discussing a work is a very good activity because it readies us for something better—reading the work. But these two activities are by no means the same. Discussing is multifaceted: the more discussants and the more varied their ideas, the better—just as long as they can pay attention to each other. Reading ultimately has just the two sides of our original dichotomy: the reader and the work. Although discussion can prepare us for reading, it is a radically different thing and no substitute for it.

The practical importance of this distinction for the teacher is its reminder that a classroom discussion is not to be confused with reading. Usually discussion results from a first assigned reading of a text; then it often precedes a second and better reading of the same text, a reading in which the student can use whatever ideas were acquired in the earlier discussion. That process can be repeated indefinitely so that we get as many alternations of reading and discussion and other helps as the students need for a full and intense command of the work.

3 Literature as Message

As we have seen, literature is both an event and an object. In that double character it also gives rise to a third aspect, a meaning. Although the meaning is imbedded in the event-object and thus not to be pulled apart from it in the completely achieved reading, still most readers, at some point in becoming acquainted with a work, like to abstract meanings; they like to talk about a work's "theme" or "subject" and to discuss a writer's "ideas" or even his "influences" and "sources" or his "intellectual milieu." This impulse to treat meaning separately from object and event can dessicate a work, but if the reader learns to put that work back together, a temporary concentration on the meaning can give a firm point of entry that allows for a degree of at-homeness; this encourages the reader to go on and explore the entire construct in its deepest levels. So, then, we may want at some point to study a work's meaning by itself, but we certainly do not want to end there.

With respect to meaning, the teacher can help the student by showing the different kinds of interest that accomplished readers take in literature—that is, the different questions they ask about it or the approaches they follow in ascertaining its meaning. Two caveats are necessary here. The first is that the following description of approaches is not a rigorously analytical taxonomy; some critics might want to add further subdivisions to the third section; and still others might want to rearrange this outline of approaches altogether. Nevertheless, the general view offered in this chapter suggests the range of interest that an experienced reader can take toward literary work, and it indicates both the sort of information that a teacher can give students in order to open a work to them, and also the questions that can be asked which will alert them to previously hidden facets of literature. The second warning that ought to be made is that this outline of approaches is merely intended for the teacher's use in finding good questions to ask and helpful information to give. It is not offered as a basis for a curriculum or as one more key for the student to memorize. Indeed, a student need not be deliberately conscious of these approaches at all. Obviously, the good reader is one who enjoys literature so much that reading it is preferable to talking about it.

The Ostensive Approach

The most direct approach to take toward literature is to read the work as a textbook about its subject. This is the normal approach to history and autobiography, to such works, for instance, as Thucydides and Gibbon, Boswell's *Life of Johnson* and Lytton Strachey's *Victorian Age*. Probably we go to these works as much for information as for specific aesthetic pleasure. Mainly the questions that we ask about works such as these are, "Does this book give the facts accurately?" and "Does the author interpret his material correctly?" Although we can hardly be indifferent to Gibbon's finely polished style or to Strachey's audacious wit, still we are chiefly interested in what they have to say about a subject that concerns us. This ostensive approach to reading involves a distinction that A. C. Bradley makes between a work's substance or content on the one hand and its subject on the other.[1] The substance is that which the work really contains within its own boundaries: Macbeth's murdering King Duncan and maneuvering himself onto the throne. The subject is that intellectual frame of reference to which the specific substance refers: in *Macbeth,* the degenerative effects of inordinate ambition. The ostensive approach emphasizes subject (what the work is about) over content (that which is distinctly within the work).

It is possible, of course, to combine an ostensive approach with other kinds of interest. Thus in *Preface to Paradise Lost,* C. S. Lewis takes a serious ostensive attitude toward Milton's theological ideas when he disputes Denis Saurat's opinion that Milton believed the reality of the universe to have resulted from God's act of withdrawing himself from a part of prime matter.[2] Lewis also attempts to contradict other interpretations by Saurat, and those who have read Lewis's books of Christian apologetics will understand that Lewis cares as much about the subject of Christian belief with which *Paradise Lost* deals as he does about the purely literary problems of interpreting Milton's words. But, at the same time, Lewis is not indifferent to Milton's art, an art which he clarifies for the reader by showing its relation to the epic genre and to the prevalent literary conventions of Milton's time.

A slightly different form that the ostensive approach to literature can take is to accept the writer as a truly great man or woman and to read the works as clear and highly charged indexes of the writer's own spiritual attainment. This was Keats's attitude to literature when he said that Shakespeare's life was a continual allegory and that his works were a commentary on it.[3] Shakespeare's life, in other words, illustrates the highest pitch of human development, and his works exist in order to help us find out what this life was really like. Thomas Carlyle viewed Shakespeare (and Dante) in the same way when he wrote "Lecture III: The Hero as Poet" in *Heroes and Hero-Worship.* John Middleton Murry, in turn, took both Shakespeare and Keats himself as exponents of spiritual striving and their works as the record of that striving in his *Keats and Shakespeare,* first published in 1925, and the several books on Keats which he produced later all resulted from his lifelong effort to penetrate ever more deeply into the mystery of moral greatness as exemplified by Keats.[4]

The Intrinsic Approach

Particularly in the form of reading the work as a spiritual account of its author, most readers find the ostensive approach an easy and natural way into fine literature, especially into those authors whom they like best. This variant of ostensive reading stands on the borderline of another kind of approach to literature, the intensive approach. Murry's attitude toward Keats assumes that the ostensible subject of "Ode to a Nightingale"—the bird itself—is not really the important aspect of the poem, which surely does not concern itself with ornithology. What does matter in the poem, Murry supposes, is the information that it gives us about states of moral consciousness which are too rare and too complex to be equally well studied by formal philosophy and psychology. Murry's view would exactly illustrate the intensive approach to reading if he were to ignore the fact of Keats's authorship of the poem, and to read "Ode to a Nightingale" without any reference to Keats's life or the conditions of Keats's time or, indeed, to anything else that is not expressed in the poem itself. In other words, whereas the ostensive approach emphasizes the work's subject—what the work is about—the intensive approach emphasizes the work's substance— what it distinctly contains within its own space.

In its most distinctive modern form—the so-called New Criticism—the intensive approach is an effort to respond to the literary work solely as an object complete in itself, and thus deliberately to ignore everything but that object. The subject insofar as it stands outside the work is ignored, the writer's character is ignored, the times in which the work was composed and the intellectual and artistic currents of those times are ignored. What is left is the "irreducibly literary," that aspect of the work which is exactly the work itself and nothing else—not the author's life, not the period in which the work was written, not even the subject of the work. To give up such help toward the understanding of a work is a large sacrifice, of course, but sometimes there are commensurate gains. Consider this little poem of Blake's.

The Sick Rose

O Rose, thou art sick!
The invisible worm
That flies in the night,
In the howling storm,

> Has found out thy bed
> Of crimson joy;
> And his dark secret love
> Does thy life destroy.

What information about Blake or about his times or about roses and worms would clarify our understanding of that poem or increase our enjoyment of it? The biographical irrelevance that Blake was very clean about himself helps us to respond to the poem much less than our observation that the brightly tangible and luxuriant rose is no match for the sneaking worm which never reveals itself except in its destructive effects.

Almost as a matter of course, we usually take the intrinsic approach to arts other than literature. Thus, when we look at a model of the Parthenon we do not worry ourselves about Pericles or the Peloponnesian War, and when we listen to Beethoven's Third Symphony we lose very little if we have never heard that story about Beethoven's first dedicating the work to Napoleon and then, denouncing Napoleon as a tyrant, tearing up the dedication page. What we need to know about the Parthenon and the Third Symphony those works themselves will tell us if we attend to them with the respect they deserve.

The intensive approach challenges our ingenuity by requiring us to focus our attention exclusively on the work we are reading and to confine ourselves to that alone. The question arises, what features of the work will grip our minds so closely that we do not slide off into extraliterary interests? The primary answer to that question is: the structure. The literature that most invites an intrinsic approach is equivocal. It takes two or more objects that arrest attention and then puts those objects through a course of complex interweavings that finally result in relationships among those objects, and between them and ourselves, which can scarcely (perhaps not at all) be stated in any other way. We have all had the experience which we express by remarking, "I know what I mean, but I can't say it." Sometimes, of course, we can't say it because we feel that we cannot take the trouble to find the right words; but sometimes, also, we can't say it because the right words do not exist. The French have an idiom for the kind of experience that cannot be formalized in ordinary discourse; they call it a *je ne sais quoi* (an "I don't know what"). Their great philosopher Pascal, a master of French prose, often uses the expression when he writes of religious experience or ethical judgment.

In "The Sick Rose," Blake takes a *je ne sais quoi* of moral conviction and expresses it, not in a formal proposition which would never convey the intuition exactly, but rather in a complex structure which invites an imaginative experience. We respond to the destructiveness of the wily, sinister worm and to the rapturous contentment of the beautiful rose.

That much of the poem we can express in ordinary prose if we take pains with it. But then Blake puts those two objects in a relationship which plain statement will surely distort. The worm, which by an instinct for destruction flies through the night and storm to kill the rose, kills it with "love," with the "dark secret love" of couples who, oblivious of all but themselves, live for each other alone. If we say in a proposition that we love something and at the same time hate it, we talk nonsense; we might as well say that we enjoyed very much the taste of a mushroom which we did not eat. When Oscar Wilde took this intuition which Blake conveys through a structure that controls our experience and tried to put it in a plain statement in his poem, "The Ballad of Reading Gaol," the best he could do was this: "Each man kills the thing he loves"—which simply is not true if taken literally and not very meaningful if taken figuratively. But if we call to mind certain intimate passages in our own lives, we shall discover in them confirmation of Blake's terrible message. Blake's poem does in fact mean intensely. But its meaning is produced in an imaginative experience which is set off by the complex structure, not in the propositions of formal, discursive language.

An essay in this book which is mainly intensive is the reading of Keats's "To Autumn." That reading detects two motives, exuberant life on the one hand and decline and death on the other, and it matches up those motives with the chief objects in the poem, with the gigantic sun and earth and with the smaller existences which those two call forth. Then the reading exposes the interrelations which the structure of the poem imposes on those motives and objects. The assumption is that one who closely follows the structure of "To Autumn" and submits to the experience which it provides will have learned something which is ineffable in ordinary language, something available only in the poem which Keats wrote and nowhere else.

The Extrinsic Approach

Certain works in particular seem to respond especially well to an intensive approach: Many of the poems of Keats, Donne, and Hopkins, for instance, invite that kind of reading, and Virginia Woolf's finely honed essay "The Death of the Moth" is an example of prose which can best be read intensively. Other works, however, including some by the writers just mentioned, need to be read with the aid of supplementary information which those works themselves do not communicate. Donne's poem "The Canonization" illustrates this fact. In a very fine and influential essay on this poem, Cleanth Brooks, who is a leading exponent of what is here called the intrinsic approach, has to go outside the poem to get a fact that helps us to read it accurately.[5] In that poem Donne defends himself, in an ironical way, against

the charge that his mistress and he are abandoned sensualists. One couplet
goes,

> Call her one, mee another flye,
> We'are Tapers too, and at our owne cost die.

All that a purely intrinsic reading would be able to make out of that word
die is that it is a vague metaphor which compares the candles' burning with
the lovers' passion. But even though Brooks mainly approaches this poem
intrinsically, at this point in his reading he brings up a linguistic fact which
the poem itself does not give but which, when we know it, greatly adds to
our understanding. *Die* was a Renaissance slang term meaning sexual
intercourse. It acquired that meaning, apparently, because of a belief current
in those times that an act of intercourse shortened by one day a person's
natural life span. Those facts about language history and old biological
fallacies enrich and specify our response to the couplet. By explaining why
Donne compares himself and his lover to lighted candles, they make a vague
and unsatisfactory metaphor become full of brilliant wit.

In Plato's *Ion,* Socrates presents the case for what can be called the
extrinsic approach to reading literature. Ion is a rhapsode; that is, his
profession is the recitation of poetry. Naturally, he thinks that he understands
Homer better than anyone else does—a prejudice which Socrates, rather
whimsically perhaps, sets out to destroy. Socrates' method is to ask who
knows most about curing disease (a physician, Ion confidently replies), about
fishing (a fisherman), and about foretelling the future (a diviner). Well,
then, Socrates asks, are there not passages in the *Iliad* that deal with curing
sickness, with fisherman, and with fortune-tellers? Ion has no answer.

Although some works can be viewed as pure intellectual forms, just as
absolute and final as circles or lines, nevertheless literature also connects
with things that are not themselves completely literary. Keats's poems, like
almost any other poet's, illustrate this difference. They can be read in
isolation from other things, or, at another time when the reader is in a
different mood perhaps, they can be read in conjunction with them. For
instance, "Ode to a Nightingale," as suggested earlier, does not treat the bird
from a realistic, biological viewpoint; it is Keats's bird, not the scientist's,
with which we should be concerned. On the other hand, Keats's poem is
not altogether a self-sufficient form; it depends on the real world in various
ways. Even his nightingale, so far transcending the scientist's that it is not
"born for death," is actually Keats's vision or revision of a real bird that flew
into the garden of a pleasant Hampstead house (still preserved) where Keats
was living with his friend Charles Brown. Brown tells the story:[6]

In the spring of 1819 a nightingale had built her nest near my house. Keats felt a tranquil and continual joy in her song; and one morning he took his chair from the breakfast-table to the grass-plot under a plum-tree, where he sat for two or three hours. When he came into the house, I perceived he had some scraps of paper in his hand, and these he was quietly thrusting behind the books. On inquiry, I found these scraps, four or five in number, contained his poetic feeling on the song of our nightingale. The writing was not well legible; and it was difficult to arrange the stanzas on so many scraps. With his assistance I succeeded, and this was his *Ode to a Nightingale,* a poem which has been the delight of everyone.

The glimpse that Brown provides of a private moment of serene content greatly enriches our feeling for the poem which that moment produced. Perhaps, even, it can do more than that; it can suggest that such a reading of "Ode to a Nightingale" as Earl R. Wasserman's, which sees the poem as a frantic alternation of despair and of struggle for happiness, is not perfectly true to Keats's experience.[7]

The extrinsic approach to literature takes facts or ideas that are not themselves literary and applies them to a work so as to illuminate our understanding of it. History, biography, psychology, sociology, and a number of other fields can all supply helpful information. Some examples will illustrate the point more clearly.

When a historical approach is used and literature is read in conjunction with events that took place at the same time it was written, our reading occasionally can be more informed than it otherwise would be. Leslie Hotson,[8] for instance, noticed that in a sonnet by Shakespeare (Number 107) there is a phrase—"the mortal moon"—which is very difficult to explicate because its literal meaning does not very well connect with the rest of the poem. Hotson pointed out the old meaning of "moone cressant" or "horned moone" as the name for a naval maneuver, a certain formation of ships at sea, and he discovered that the Spanish Armada used that maneuver during its foray against England in 1588. Shakespeare's line "The mortal moon has suffered her eclipse" Hotson thought could be paraphrased as "The Spanish Armada has been defeated." Therefore, Hotson concluded, the poem was probably written not long after the attempted invasion, and as a result of that argument he placed the composition of at least some of Shakespeare's sonnets at a date earlier than the one customarily given. Whether or not he is right about the date of the sonnet, his historical exploration allows us to make sense of a line that would merely tease and irritate us if we did not have that information. This sonnet and others become much clearer and more specific in the light of contemporary events to which they apparently allude.

Another instance where Shakespeare's writing is clarified by history is the book *The Royal Play of Macbeth* by Henry N. Paul.[9] Paul tells us that James I, who formerly had been King of Scotland only, had just mounted the throne of England and that *Macbeth* was, among other things, Shakespeare's compliment to the new king. That fact explains a number of features in the play. There is a scene for instance, in which Macbeth visits the witches a second time in order to ask them if he will have sons who will become kings. For answer, the witches present a visionary procession which shows that he will have no successors to inherit the crown, but that from Banquo will stem an endless line of kings ("What!" Macbeth asks, "Will the line stretch out to the crack of doom?" [IV, i, 117]) and some of them will carry triple scepters. When we are told that James believed himself to be descended from Banquo, this dumb-show of a long line of monarchs wearing triple crowns we understand as a graceful allusion to James's long, distinguished ancestry and to the fact that he was the first of his family to become King of England and (by pretension) France, as well as King of Scotland.

A special kind of historical study of literature is called the History of Ideas. This approach assumes that every historical epoch is characterized by certain prevailing ideas about things, and that throughout that epoch these ideas are so widespread and so firmly held as to have the force of undisputed axioms from which people confidently derive other ideas. Thus, in the period of the Enlightenment (late seventeenth century and eighteenth century) educated Western Europeans almost universally believed that those religious, philosophic, and political opinions were most likely to be true which had been believed by most men in most places and times. This conception, which was a deeply ingrained notion in that period, supported a number of eighteenth century convictions: the belief, for instance, that one's opinions had better be moderate rather than eccentrically novel or fantastically old-fashioned. ("Be not the first by whom the new is tried / Nor yet the last to lay the old aside.") Perhaps a more notable outcropping of the idea that what is most probably true is that which most people in most times and places have believed is the ardor for democracy which grew up in the eighteenth century and culminated in the American and French Revolutions. A political election in which all citizens have an equal vote is, after all, nothing but a systematic way of discovering what most persons in most places (within a given country) believe, and the American constitutional framers at any rate, by interphasing the election of president, senators, and representatives, tried to spread the consensus over a fairly ample stretch of time.

The History of Ideas approach has been employed by a number of distinguished scholars. A. O. Lovejoy, in his seminal book *The Great Chain of Being,*[10] examined the leading ideas of the Enlightenment and traced those ideas in the writing of the time. His masterful essay "On the Discrimination of Romanticisms" is still being respectfully read fifty years after its original publication.[11] V. L. Parrington's *Main Currents in American Thought*[12] connects American ideas with American literature, though in a way that seems to exalt second-rate artistic production over major authors and works. M. H. Abrams' *The Mirror and the Lamp*[13] studies the connection between general sensibility and the change in outlook upon literature which took place all over Europe and America during the late eighteenth and early nineteenth centuries. In his persuasive and neatly expressed *The Active Universe,* H. W. Piper[14] examines the influence on Wordsworth and Coleridge of religious, political, and scientific ideas which circulated in their day. Alice Chandler's *A Dream of Order*[15] is an illuminating book which shows the impact that a rather sentimental view of the Middle Ages had on a number of Romantic and Victorian writers. Many other book-length studies and the quarterly *Journal of the History of Ideas* attest to the continuing vitality of this approach.

An advantage which the History of Ideas approach gives to the reading and teaching of literature is that it helps to specify the content of works, to make more apparent to us the intellectual component of those works, and thus to aid us in fixing our minds on something substantial. These famous lines from Pope's *Essay on Man* (Epistle II, lines 1–19) will illustrate the point:

> Know then thyself, presume not God to scan;
> The proper study of Mankind is Man.
> Plac'd on this isthmus of a middle state,
> A Being darkly wise and rudely great:
> With too much knowledge for the Sceptic side,
> With too much weakness for the Stoic's pride,
> He hangs between; in doubt to act, or rest,
> In doubt to deem himself a God, or beast;
> In doubt his Mind or Body to prefer;
> Born but to die, and reas'ning but to err;
> Alike in ignorance, his reason such,
> Whether he thinks too little, or too much:
> Chaos of Thought and Passion, all confus'd;
> Still by himself abus'd, or disabus'd;
> Created half to rise, and half to fall;
> Great lord of all things, yet a prey to all;
> Sole judge of Truth, in endless error hurl'd;
> The glory, jest, and riddle of the world!

We can read that passage and get only a general and indistinct impression of neat rhymes that, through paradoxes, suggest the indeterminate nature of human beings, neither gods nor beasts, and their resulting hesitation and insufficiency. On the other hand, if we go to Lovejoy's *Great Chain of Being,* we shall find there an account of an idea that dominated Renaissance and

Augustan thought and which works its way into Pope's lines so as to give them specific meaning. The notion of the so-called great chain of being is that every possibility of created existence does in fact exist, and that all separate existences are arranged and linked with each other on a line of continual modification, from the simple atom up to God himself. Humankind is one of those links in the whole cosmic organization, and within the smaller human community each person is higher or lower than another and thus linked into a total society. Both as an occupant of the complexly ordered universe and as a member of human culture, a human being has the ethical business to "know itself," to know its place.

When we read Pope against the backdrop of contemporary thought that gets into his writing, his poetry gives us something definite that we can respond to. We more clearly perceive ideas that really are in the poem, not just irrelevant thoughts of our own, and we begin to understand why Pope writes about such ideas in an antithetical manner. In short, the poem begins to come together for us. More than that, if we decide to teach this passage, we shall have some precise intellectual content. We shall have definite points to convey to our students, if we lecture, or to aim to elicit from them if we prefer more inductive methods of teaching.

Another form of the extrinsic approach to literature is biographical. Like other artists, writers lead unusually interesting lives, and we would want to know about their circumstances and behavior even if that knowledge did not help us to read their works more insightfully. To a large audience Byron and F. Scott Fitzgerald seem to be as interesting in themselves as they are in their works. We all want to know the secret of genius, literary as well as other kinds, and so we read authors' works to find out, if we can, what that secret is. Beyond satisfying our curiosity about the great, however, literary biography has more practical uses in guiding and strengthening our reading. In reference to Charles Dickens, for example, it was pointed out long ago that one of his most famous characters, David Copperfield, had as his initials Dickens's own, reversed, and that young Copperfield, like Dickens himself in his childhood, worked in a blacking warehouse for a brief period, and that Mr. Micawber's irresponsibility, manic temperament, and incarceration for debt all applied to Dickens's own father.

If the connections between Dickens's life and his work amounted only to these similarities, then his biography would hardly be of help to us in comprehending his novels. Not all the relations between the life and the work are superficial, however. Some of them are important. From what Dickens told his biographer Forster about his time in the blacking warehouse, for instance, we know that this brief episode in his life, which most men would have repressed or at least recalled without horror, was for him a genuine trauma.[16] Years after the event he could not bring himself to go near the part of London where the warehouse had stood. Dickens's obsession with the episode seems, in part, to betray the social insecurity of a Victorian bourgeois and also to express a deeper personal insecurity that Dickens himself associated with the occasional poverty and the constant financial anxiety of his childhood.

These inferences about Dickens's character help us to read his novels. Dickens's social uneasiness alerts us, for instance, to his lower-middle-class, pounds-and-pence point of view that tells the cost of everything and delights in clean old men like Wemick's father (in *Great Expectations*) and the Brothers Cheeryble (in *Nicholas Nickleby*). They show that Miss Havisham's unkempt get-up and her rotten wedding cake express Dickens's horror of her, and that Mr. Boffin, the Golden Dustman of *Our Mutual Friend,* is associated either with the bright comeliness of his wife or with heaps of garbage, according to the role, benign or malignant, that he happens to be playing at the moment. Dickens's personal insecurity contributes the basic plot situation of most of his novels: an abandoned child (whether rich or poor) in search of adults who will love him.

In this biographical approach to Dickens that we have just sketched, there is nothing that is new to Dickens scholars and little that is controversial. Some might want to add or modify details, but in outline the viewpoint given above is generally acceptable. In a different instance, in which interpretations of a writer's life are disputed, the biographical approach can still help our reading, although in a different way. Thomas Hardy illustrates the point. In 1966 two scholars, Lois Deacon and Terry Coleman, thinking that they had unearthed some facts about Hardy that shed light on his temperament and writing, published a book, *Providence and Mr. Hardy,*[17] which aroused much discussion and controversy. They think they have evidence to show that in his early twenties Thomas Hardy had a love affair with a young woman, Tryphena Sparks, that the two were engaged, and that the engagement was abruptly broken off, even though Tryphena shortly afterwards bore Hardy a son. After breaking the engagement, the two went their different ways into separate marriages. According to Deacon and Coleman, the explanation of these events is that whereas Hardy at first thought that Tryphena was his cousin, he discovered after the engagement (and the beginning of Tryphena's pregnancy) that she actually was his neice. He had, unknowingly, committed incest, and that enormity was the source of the enduring pessimism which he expressed repeatedly in his poems, novels, and stories. It may be that only some of these interpretations are true, or possibly even none is true.[18] But true or false, the book by Deacon and Coleman brings us back to the essential thing in Hardy's work, his tragic outlook. Their book forces us to come to grips with Hardy's unique temperament and with the subtle and moving expressions of it. After reading Deacon and Coleman we may disagree with their detective work, but we shall be grateful to them for having directed our attention to the basic Hardy: the troubled, somber, and compassionate man who felt life to be an infliction too heavy to bear.

Literature can also be studied by applying to it information and theories that come from the field of psychology. This application can be made in various ways. One way is to try to recount readers' transactions with texts, the interplay between the individual reader, with his or her own beliefs, cares, and experience, on the other hand, with the particular literary work on the other. A pioneer in this and other fields of study is I. A. Richards. In *Principles of Literary Criticism*[19] he laid down a theoretical base for examining response to literature, and in *Practical Criticism*[20] he investigated in considerable detail the ways in which readers deal with poetry. The central idea of *Principles of Literary Criticism* is that an art work, in contrast to other kinds of stimuli, has two notable effects upon its audience. In the first place, it unleashes an unusually large number of diverse nerve impulses. Second, it coordinates all those impulses with each other so as to produce a response that is pleasurably harmonious. This harmonization of many heterogeneous impulses is a healthy thing, Richards believes, and it constitutes the high value of art. Ordinary life, with its unresolved conflicts, its disappointments, and repressions, inevitably unsettles our psychic organization (who can drive through city traffic or listen to the evening news without becoming furious?), but art restores it. Hence the "correct" reading of a work is the one that allows that work to call out many different responses and then goes on to blend those responses into a total, unified reaction.

In *Practical Criticism* the empirical base which Richards used for his report of readers' responses to poetry was a large number of frank, written reactions ("protocols" Richards called them) which he taught his audience—mainly Cambridge University undergraduates—to compose. In the presentation of his findings Richards systematically groups these protocols into the different kinds of faults that can inhibit correct reading, and thus he illustrates such failures as idiosyncratic associations, stock responses, and sentimentality. He takes thirteen poems, and in discussing the readers' protocols he shows not only what were the values and the faults in their responses but also what a right reading of each of the poems is. On both counts, on the criticism of the protocols and on the readings of the poems, Richards is very persuasive, and teachers who are unwilling to be browbeaten by students (or certain critics) who say that any sincere reading of a work is as good as another will find much comfort in Richards's book.

A more recent researcher in this field of response to literature is Norman Holland. Basing himself on Freudian (and post-Freudian) psychoanalysis, Holland charts in his book *Dynamics of Literary Response*[21] what he considers to be the main lines of communication between literary texts and readers. Holland agrees that one of these lines is artistic apprehension; he regards himself as a so-called new critic and he has no fault to find, at least in principle, with the kind of criticism illustrated by the remarks on Blake's "The Sick Rose" which appeared earlier in this chapter. But he is mainly interested in another line of communication, with the subconscious dealings that readers have with literary works. He thinks that literature arouses libidinal impulses which would offend a reader if they were known but which are cut off from entering the conscious by certain defenses (denial, displacement, reaction formation, and the rest) which literature also stimulates. Thus, Holland thinks that both the "Tomorrow and tomorrow and tomorrow" speech in *Macbeth* and also Matthew Arnold's "Dover Beach" arouse a primal scene fantasy—an unconscious memory of seeing our parents in sexual intercourse and mistaking the event as the father's beating the mother. But Holland feels that those works are structured so as not only to arouse this fantasy but also to allay it.

In *Poems in Persons*,[22] Holland modifies his earlier view somewhat—and takes a long step toward subjective solipsism. Holland begins by describing the analysis of the poet "H. D." (Hilda Doolittle) by Freud himself. Then he examines a poem of hers to show that it accords with the character of the woman who made it. Last, he shows that the responses of three different readers (himself and two college student volunteers) accord, not with the poem, but rather with *their* separate characters. Holland concludes that each person "poems his own poem."[23] My meat is your poison. The effect of his argument is to deny that a work has much control over a reader's response, especially at deep levels of personality.[24]

Not everyone who knows literature will be willing to go the whole length of Holland's argument. Some will probably feel that he does not weight heavily enough the conscious factors that help to make up a response to a literary work. Others, noting that his study is not longitudinal, may think that he makes insufficient allowance for the possibility that a literary work determines for us the right response if we live with it long enough—if, as Keats says, we "wander with it, and muse upon it, and reflect upon it, and bring home to it, and prophesy upon it, and dream upon it."[25] Nonetheless, much of what Holland says certainly conforms with our experience of literature. He is right to point out that we must ultimately rely upon our own particular selves in order to apprehend a work and that those selves differ widely from each other. Holland can teach us something about the subjective side of literary response.

Alan Purves has contributed to the scholarly discussion of response to literature by categorizing the kinds of statements that can be made about a work.[26] Purves sets up five main divisions—engagement, perception, interpretation, evaluation, and miscellaneous—and then subdivides those divisions into one hundred and twenty different kinds of statements that are possible. His scheme has the virtue of clarity, and it gives a basis for research efforts that need definitions of responses that are to be investigated. But his divisions are more logical than real. Our response to a work is one whole reaction, not five. Furthermore, not all responses to literature can be couched in Purves's categories of expression. There is that *je ne sais quoi* mentioned earlier, and probably for most of us the most cherishable response is the one that we cannot put into words.

The teacher who investigates the writings of Richards, Holland, and Purves will find there much that can be used in improving literature classes. From Richards there is a comprehensible and remarkably sane explanation of response to literature, and, perhaps even more useful, there are in Richards's protocols many examples of responses that are articulate and interesting and which students themselves can analyze. Holland elucidates some of the underground happenings that go into our thoughts and feelings about literature, and in *Poems in Persons* especially he has some good hints for teaching readers to identify the personal factors that influence their reactions. Purves adumbrates the wide range of possible responses to literary works.

A second application of psychology to literature—and perhaps more common—is the explanation of a work's meaning by resort to psychological principles of behavior. Sometimes a critic will take fictional characters, as if they were real people subject to ordinary laws of behavior, and treat them as case studies illustrating human adjustment. Thus we speak of Captain Ahab's fixations of all his hatreds and anxieties upon the whale and compare his psychological development to Starbuck, who seems to have a surer grasp on reality; we relate Madame Bovary's unrealistic expectations concerning her love affairs to the escapist and erotic literature which she had read as a school girl; and we see in Silas Marner the radical reformation of character through the agency of love. A slightly different way of elucidating the meaning of a work is to read it as an analyst interprets his patient's dreams, and thus to see it as an expression of its author's psychic state. An example of this manner of reading is Sir Ernest Jones's very influential interpretation of *Hamlet,* which he takes as an expression of Shakespeare's inability to work through the Oedipal crisis and achieve a satisfactory adjustment to his father.[27] Thus the play turns on Hamlet's grief for the safely dead old king, on whom he can lavish affection with no threat of rejection, and on Hamlet's detestation of the foster father, Claudius, who enacts with Hamlet's mother a role which Hamlet himself would fulfill were it not for his repression. Perhaps Jones's study also illustrates the danger which Freudian critics face of being vulgarized. The Laurence Olivier film version of *Hamlet,* though superficially resembling Jones's, seems really to be based on a common misunderstanding of what orthodox Freudians consider the Oedipus complex to be. Unlike Jones's Hamlet, Olivier's is a victim of conscious incestuous desires, and in the bedroom scene he glances longingly from his mother to her bed in an unintentional comic parody of Jones's interpretations.

The twentieth century has produced many psychoanalytical studies that discover the personal qualities of authors through analysis of their works. One such study is Edmund Wilson's *The Wound and the Bow: Seven Studies in Literature.*[28] His essays on Dickens, Kipling, and Joyce are especially rewarding, and they illustrate the largeness of outlook that can be attained by a psychological critic who is not wedded to any one particular school of psychology. Marie Bonaparte produced an intriguing and persuasive study of Poe.[29] Frederic Crews, who masters several approaches to literature, tempers and corrects his psychological insights with alternative viewpoints. His "Conrad's Uneasiness—and Ours"[30] is a subtle blending of outlooks which avoids the narrow reductionism of much psychoanalytic criticism.

C. J. Jung's theories, especially his notion of a racial or collective unconscious, have been made the basis of still another psychological approach to literature—myth criticism or archetypal criticism, as it is called. Jung observes that certain images are universal; they appear in everyone's fantasies, and, moreover, they conform to widely circulated myths. Those myths and the images with which they correspond, Jung supposes, are the individual's most intimate connection with the whole life of mankind outside himself. In her book *Archetypal Patterns in Poetry,* Maud Bodkin takes these ideas and applies them to the analysis of literature.[31] She finds that certain great works which she studies—from Milton's *Paradise Lost* to Eliot's *The Waste Land* and Lawrence's *Women in Love*—repeat figures and situations that incessantly appear in folklore, myth, and classical literature, and she concludes that those figures and situations are indeed archetypal: They have their peculiar power over us because they express memories of ours which reach far out and far back from our private selves.

Whatever objections some readers of literature might have to archetypal criticism on the ground that it is a misty and weak substitute for religion, one support for the myth critics seems unassailable—that is, the peculiar imaginative power of certain ubiquitous images which "vibrate in the memory." Rivers that must be crossed, gods and heroes who sacrifice themselves for their inferiors, servants and animals that are unswervingly faithful, and a number of other such recurrent images seem to elicit feelings that are very powerful and are the same for all of us, and which we would prefer not to express in straightforward, unambiguous language. Some myth critics have succeeded better than others in locating those motives that exert an unusual power and in deciphering their meaning. Certainly one of the most accomplished of such critics is Dorothy Van Ghent; her little book on

Willa Cather helps to make us receptive to the impact of Cather's best work, and it shows why Cather's novels are deeply moving.[32]

In the 'fifties and thereafter, a variant on the idea of myth criticism arose. Whereas such critics as Bodkin and Van Ghent dealt with literature as an outcropping of a rather mysterious "collective unconscious," others like Northrop Frye and Leslie Fiedler added to the original idea the notion that literature also embodies group aspirations and identifications that are socially inculcated, sentiments that pervade a whole culture or subculture and set it off from other groups. Fiedler tries to define this new and expanded idea of myth in his fine essay on *Huckleberry Finn*, " 'Come Back to the Raft Ag'in, Huck Honey.' "

> I hope I have been using here a hopelessly abused word with some precision: by "archetype" I mean a coherent pattern of beliefs and feelings so widely shared at a level beneath consciousness that there exists no abstract vocabulary for representing it, and so "sacred" that unexamined, irrational restraints inhibit any explicit analysis. Such a complex finds a formula or pattern story, which serves both to embody it, and, at first at least, to conceal its full implications. Later, the secret may be revealed, the archetype "analyzed" or "allegorically" interpreted according to the language of the day.[33]

Northrop Frye's theory about the way in which literature connects social surroundings with the individual consciousness can be gathered from his essay "The Critical Path: An Essay on the Social Context of Literature."[34] In an approach that sees literature in an enormous context of cultural development and process, Frye points out that cultures base themselves on one set of beliefs, "myths of concern"—or that which it concerns everyone within a given culture to believe so as to preserve that culture—but that they also eventually spawn another set, "myths of freedom"—those less primitive ideas that extend one's intellectual grasp beyond mere acceptance of social duties, toward enlightened comparison, criticism, and analysis. Like religion and political ideology, literature mainly serves to inculcate myths of concern; it incarnates the convictions that identify a culture and help individuals to find themselves within that culture. Frye's notion of "literature" is wide, much more inclusive than most English teachers' certainly, and he sees no hope for objective evaluation of literature, nor, for that matter, does he treat literature as a fine art to be contemplated just for its own sake. Anyone who disagrees with Frye's denigration of the "idolatry of art"[35] will nonetheless find good intellectual exercise in trying to state those objections to Frye's briskly argued position.

Both Fiedler and Frye relate literature to the cultural matrix from which it grows, even though they also see it in other connections as well. It is not a very great distance from them to other critics who concentrate more directly on the social environment of literature, the sociological critics. Such a critic, who always has interesting things to say about modern literature, is Malcolm Cowley, whose *Exile's Return* enlivens our understanding of the great American literary works of the 'twenties by showing the influence on them of post-World War I social conditions.[36] Although the polymathic Edmund Wilson is too far-ranging an intellect to be confined to any one approach to art, his *To the Finland Station*[37] mainly follows a sociological line in examining the radical thought that animated American literature in the 'twenties and 'thirties, and his *Axel's Castle*[38] examines the supranational artistic milieu of the period between 1879 and 1930. Alfred Kazin is another compendious intellect, but the sociological bent of his view of literature is shown in the title of his richly stocked and finely expressed *On Native Grounds*.[39]

By nature sociologists are theorizers, and since a widespread theory among them is Marxism, many critics who take a sociological approach to literature have drawn upon Marxian theory in their interpretations and evaluations. Some of these critics, like Georg Lukács and Christopher Caudwell,[40] are avowed Communists who consciously link their literary theories to Communist Party ideology and to its "socialist realistic" requirement that art discourage bourgeois attitudes and offer idealized but at the same time credible models of socially responsible behavior. Other critics in this group treat Marx's ideas academically, applying them when they seem appropriate to the discussion of literary works but reserving political allegiance. One of the most adept of such critics is Lionel Trilling, who borrows from Marx just as he also taxes Freud and other thinkers to combine all those ideas with his own astute reading and keen observation so as to form a civilized and instructed sensibility.

It would be possible to extend this survey still farther. We could examine critics, for instance, who delve into ethics and then apply ethical principles to the analysis of literature, or we could look at the critics who explore the relations—very illuminating some of them—between literature and the other arts, between literature and music, literature and dance, literature and painting. For that matter, the relations between literature and science can often be studied fruitfully.

The Message and Teaching

In fact we have gone far enough in this survey to make the main point. That point is this: Teachers of literature do not have to confine themselves to the kind of question that runs, "Who did what to whom on the bottom of page thirty?" The teacher who is equipped with an understanding of the

variety of interests which literature can gratify has access to a large range of
questions that can be used to provoke and sustain students' curiosity. Any
work will do for illustrating this point, but take as an example this much
anthologized lyric by W. B. Yeats.

> When You Are Old
>
> When you are old and grey and full of sleep,
> And nodding by the fire, take down this book,
> And slowly read, and dream of the soft look
> Your eyes had once, and of their shadows deep.
>
> How many loved your moments of glad grace,
> And loved your beauty with love false or true.
> But one man loved the pilgrim soul in you,
> And loved the sorrows of your changing face;
>
> And bending down beside the glowing bars,
> Murmur, a little sadly, how Love fled
> And paced upon the mountains overhead
> And hid his face amid a crowd of stars.

Trying to look at that poem in the light of the various approaches that
can be taken to literature suggests questions such as the following:

Ostensive approach questions:

1. Is it inevitable that we want more happiness out of our lives than
   we can possibly get?
2. Is it true that men and women who love ideals necessarily lose the
   love of other humans?

Intrinsic approach questions:

1. Was the woman to whom the poem is addressed young or old when
   the poem was written?
2. Is the poem in any way threatening to the woman?
3. Why is *Love* capitalized? Does the word refer in any degree to the
   author himself?
4. How could a man love a woman's "pilgrim soul" but nevertheless
   be called to things such as "mountains overhead" and the "crowd of
   stars"? To what do those metaphors allude?

Extrinsic approach questions:

1. (Historical) What was Ireland's relation to England at the time this
   poem was written?

2. (History of ideas) How does the spirit of nationalism enter into this love poem?

3. (Biographical) Who was Maud Gonne? What relation did she have to Yeats?

4. (Psychological) Is this a poem by a man who is in love or rather a poem by one who thinks he would like to be in love? Does the poem in any way punish the woman? Would it be altogether flattering to receive such a poem? Which words come nearest to describing your feelings after you have comprehended the poem— *bitterness, strain, sadness, joy, comfort, satisfaction, regret, fear, hopelessness?* Are any other words better than these?

5. (Archtypal) Who was Kathleen ni Hoolihan? Does Maud Gonne, as she is presented here, accord better with Kathleen than she does with Miss Liberty or Britannia?

6. (Sociological) Does the wording of the poem allow you to make any guesses as to the social and economic status of the man and woman? What types of men might be able to feel the emotions that are expressed in this poem? What types would be less apt to feel these emotions?

A teacher who wanted to present this poem to students would have here a number of questions representing different entrances into the work. No teacher would care to use all these questions, although different teachers— quite rightly—would reject different questions. Certain questions on this list would be uncongenial with certain teachers, others might be irrelevant for certain students or classes, and of course some are not central to the work. (The sociological questions seem to me to miss the heart of this particular poem by a long way.)

But even though the teacher in any given situation will omit some of the questions, still a large supply of them helps instruction. A generous backlog gives many advantages. The teacher can choose out of it what is just right for teacher and students alike, and since in teaching we can rarely predict exactly what will find students' sensibilities, we need to feel along many dimensions of a work in order to bring it within the separate ranges of different students who have different aptitudes and different susceptibilities. Finally, since a good work is always a rich work, never simple in the sense that it properly elicits just a single, unmodified response, the teacher wants to help students to react to its many-sidedness, and therefore asks many questions rather than just a few.

4 What Is a Good Reading?

The material in the foregoing chapters may be enough to establish a point of view from which we can try to answer the question, what is a good reading of a literary work? That question is controversial, of course, and answers to it will vary according to differences of opinion about what literature is and what it does. What I mean by a "good" reading has already been implied, I hope, but now I shall try to be explicit.

If we find a satisfactory definition of a good reading, are we then in a position to evaluate any particular reading—our own, a professional critic's, or (most important from a teacher's point of view) a student's—and say of it that it is good or not good or somewhere in between? A little reflection suggests that we cannot give a single and definitive yes or no answer to that question. But if we examine the question in a tentative and candid spirit, we may come up with partial answers that will suggest some useful principles for making our evaluation of students a little less odious and a little more fair.

Like all the arts, literature is an event-object-message; it simultaneously presents to the reader three different sets of stimuli: an interior happening to experience, a palpable thing to observe, and a significance to ponder. A reading that accords with these three facets in a literary work will itself possess three corresponding features: intensity, order, and abundance.

The feature of intensity in the reader's reception answers to the work as an event, as a happening within the consciousness. Intensity is the almost fevered fascination that we allude to when we say that a work is compelling or gripping. A story which I. A. Richards tells about some reading that he did aptly illustrates the nature of intensity.[1] As Richards was sitting outdoors under a tree, he read an account by Captain Slocum (the first person to sail around the earth single-handed) of being bitten on the head by a centipede while along in the middle of the Atlantic. Just at that moment, a falling leaf hit Richards in the face, and, his feelings suddenly released, he leaped out of his chair.

Of the three features that characterize a good reading, intensity seems to be the one that is both the most difficult to reduce to particular behavioral manifestations and yet the most easy to recognize. For instance, some of Samuel Johnson's remarks on *Paradise Lost*, including his ironic comment that "None ever wished it longer than it is," raise a doubt whether he read that particular work intensely.[2] On the other hand, Boswell's wonderful anecdotes about Johnson's literary conversation and his own *Lives of the English Poets* and other critical writings reveal a sensibility that normally was all afire with excitement and concentrated attention. Johnson himself gave us the clue for discovering the presence of intensity. "No man is a hypocrite in his pleasures," he once remarked.[3] Aesthetic intensity is so hard to fake that in a scholarly journal one can find two articles side by side and, without being able to specify the evidence, know that the one article was written out of love of the work under discussion and the other was produced from some other motive—an interest in ideas for their own sake, for instance, or a desire to illustrate some thesis about group behavior or the transmission of culture.

But if we must have behavioral signs of intensity, what should we look for? One convincing sign is a person's reading literature voluntarily, for few people will keep up a schedule of active reading if they do not cherish literature. But the crucial indication is the alacrity to read literature, not the sheer volume of reading; it is a delusion to suppose that a large quantity of desultory reading is equal to the close study of particular works. Stories circulate about famous people who read omnivorously, up to a book a day. But such a reading schedule as that merely indicates a compulsion neurosis, not aesthetic intensity; it has more to do with turning pages than with reading them. When we read literature intensely we try to get *into* the book, not *through* it. Thus the kind of voluntary reading the teacher should look for is in the student who freely returns to a work, either by rereading it or by revising his or her adjustment to it as it sinks deeper into the student's consciousness, or by comparing and contrasting it with other works.

Other signs of intensity will derive from this willingness to read. Since an intense reading is always deeply felt, the student who has read intensely will probably want to talk about the work, for most of us like to explain to others the experiences that have strongly moved us. This observation, of course, is only true in general, and teachers will be able to think of students who would rather not talk about experiences that have affected them. Even so, fewer people will be reluctant to write about those experiences, and no one will be indifferent to hearing others discuss them and add information about them. As a consequence, the teacher can be pretty sure that if an informative lesson has been arranged about a work which the class has read, the students who take part (either by speaking or by listening acutely) have read the work intensely and those who are bored by the lesson were also bored by the work.

To get a clearer sense of what order in reading literature is, we need to go back for a moment to the reading episode which Richards relates. The accident of the leaf's unleashing Richards's vivid feelings illustrates the intensity that is indispensable in a good reading, and in fact that accident exposed intensity in its pure state, unmodified by order or abundance. Richards's reading was faulty, however, because it did not have all the necessary qualities. Up to the point that the leaf struck him, Richards was able to contain his feelings where they belonged—within himself. But the falling leaf so surprised him that he suddenly lost the distinction between the art work and life itself and, in a temporary delusion, mixed the two together. Richards's failures were his momentarily forgetting that the book conveyed an inner, not an outer, happening, and his behaving as if the situation presented in the book were actual at that moment rather than imagined.

Richards's faulty reading exemplifies a failure in order. Order in our reception of a work is the exact accommodation of the mind to all the specificities of the work which cause it to be the particular object that it is. The quality of order in a reading is perhaps analogous to *responsiveness* as lawyers use that term (in television serials at least) when they speak of legal testimony. Consider this dialogue.

Lawyer: Where were you the night of June 23?

Witness: Watching television.

Lawyer: *Where* were you?

Witness: With my girl friend.

Lawyer: Your Honor, the witness is not responsive.

Just as the witness was able to give answers that were relevant to the question but not responsive, so readers of a literary work can receive it in ways that are relevant but not ordered. The student who, desperate to make some kind of sense of G. M. Hopkins's poem "Pied Beauty," spoke of it as "Pie-Eyed Beauty" failed notably in order, for rather than submit to Hopkins's meaning, which could have been discovered by consulting a dictionary, the student's own meaning was imposed instead. Until that student learns to make ordered readings, literature will be only a mirror that reflects back the student's own preconceptions, not a window through which to look out at experiences that are new and different. At a simpler level this student was making essentially the same kind of disordered reading that, on a sophisticated plane, the psychoanalytic critic makes by reducing an entire complex work by Conrad to castration anxiety or that a Marxist critic makes by reducing the same work to a message denouncing capitalistic exploitation. Probably the student who misread Hopkins will mend his or her ways, but the two critics, their minds clouded by partial illumination, are likely to go on forever reading works and seeing nothing in them but castration anxiety or capitalistic exploitation.

Attaining order seems to be more difficult for readers than achieving intensity. Perhaps the reason is that intensity grows directly and inevitably out of an experience, whatever it happens to be, whereas order requires that we deliberately and painstakingly adjust ourselves to a given fact. Intense feeling comes to us more easily than ordered observation. In reading literature we must have them both, however. If intensity tends toward the excitement and vividness of experience, order yields the specificity and particularity of disciplined observation. By itself, intensity is just another name for frenzy, and order alone is mere attention; together, combined with abundance, they give us the passionate serenity of aesthetic delight.

Order in the reading relates to structure in the work. As objects, literary works are highly structured, but their structure is not like the simple form of a lump of coal; rather it is like the intricate organization in a leaf or in a human body. Instead of manifesting just one principle of organization, the literary work may arise out of multiple sets of interrelated systems. In my reading of Keats's "To Autumn" (Chapter VI) I have tried to expose the multiform structure that supports the work: There is the cyclical structure given by the season as it moves from late summer to early winter; there is the related, faster progression of a single day as it goes from dawn to twilight; there is an organization of impulses that glide from birth through harvest into death; there is a counterpointing of near and far, intimate and vast; and comprehending all these there is the metaphoric comparison of the universe with a loving family.

We can agree that an ordered reading will adjust itself to the structure(s) of the work. Probably we shall also agree that in specific instances this general principle will have to be applied with latitude. For one thing, serious readers sometimes differ in their assessments of what the basic structures are—though, more often than not, these disagreements really have to do with the wording of interpretations or with a confusion of a work's content with its subject matter, rather than a major difference in two readers' constituting of the work itself. More important, few works, even great ones, are perfect in the sense that their structures fully realize themselves. *Hamlet, Moby Dick,* Shelley's *Prometheus Unbound* are masterpieces, of course, but their structures are flawed, for their greatness rests in the grand scope of moral implication for which a tightly knit structure is hardly possible. In these cases the reader must, by fellow-feeling with the author and the work, complete inwardly through constituting what the artist could not entirely achieve in the outward manifestation.

The principle that an ordered reading bases itself on the structure of the work does not mean that the reader must consciously identify that structure. Just as a music amateur can hear a modulation perfectly well without knowing what it is or how, technically, it is produced, so a reader can be open to the influence of structure and yet be unable to analyze it. In our own reading we have all seen illustrations of this fact in the works that captivate us beyond any power of ours to explain in a formal analysis. I have found that many lyrics by Shelley and long sections of *Walden* invariably exert upon me a fascination that far exceeds my conscious comprehension of the works themselves. Sometimes it also happens that a reading deliberately takes up one of the structures in a work but does not consciously embrace others. "To Autumn" is a case in point. Most readers will see in that poem the cycles of the progressing season and the lengthening day, but fewer will be aware of the concatenation of images into a pattern of birth-harvest-death, and still fewer will notice the implied comparison of the universe with a family until it is pointed out to them. But even when readers detect only part of the structure, the rest may well be available to them at a level beneath conscious articulation. This is not really a mystery, or at least if it is, it is certainly not confined to art. The same intuitive, inarticulate grasp of a thing is acting when we sense, on the basis of evidence that we could not put into words, that one student in a class is unusually happy that day and that another has just done something he should not have done. Pascal, intrepid adventurer in the *je ne sais quoi,* has expressed this point succinctly: "The heart has its reasons which Reason does not know." And in the beginning pages of *Les Pensées* he has carefully exposed the essential distinction between artistic and scientific temperaments as consisting in the different ways that these two establish order in their respective domains: The artistic temperament intuitively grasps in a single glimpse the order that inheres in a vast number of details, whereas the scientific temperament deliberately outlines order by sorting out the details through the painstaking application of general rules.

A reading will give certain signs that it is ordered. First of all, an ordered reading will constitute the details of a work accurately; it will be filled both with primary sense perceptions of objects, sounds, temperatures, and also with intuitions of emotional atmosphere that derive from those perceptions. Consider the amount and variety of such constitutings that are stimulated by the beginning lines of Edwin Arlington Robinson's "The Man Against the Sky":

> Between me and the sunset, like a dome
> Against the glory of a world on fire,
> Now burned a sudden hill,
> Bleak, round, and high, by flame-lit height made higher,
> With nothing on it for the flame to kill
> Save one who moved and was alone up there
> To loom before the chaos and the glare
> As if he were the last god going home
> Unto his last desire.

An ordered reading of these lines will begin by recognizing two violent contrasts in physical sensation: the one between the height of the hill against the lowness of the place where Robinson stands; the other between the scorching red light that outlines the hill versus the darkness that blots out the flat below. The scene is a lurid, grotesque clashing of high and low, red and black.

An ordered reading not only constitutes the details accurately; it also puts those details together in a comprehensiveness that allows a passage to become whole by uniting its parts into a total impression. In an ordered reading of Robinson's lines, for instance, the primary sensations lead to impressions of earthquake and conflagration. To this feeling-tone of universal cataclysm an ordered reading will adjust the solitary figure that stands high up in the blaze of universal destruction, and out of these components it will intuit Robinson's idea of the world we live in—the cursed and dying world of the *Niebelungenlied* and the *Götterdämmerung* where the gods themselves ultimately fulfill their wish to die.

This putting together of the details into a whole object requires that the reader search the work for principles of organization. For instance, in reading the lines from Robinson's poem we have related the details to each other by supposing that there is a tacit allusion to Wagner's *Ring* and the Norse mythology from which it borrows. Once we sense that allusion, then many of the details fall into place—the wide and open perspective of landscape, the collapse of the universe, the god yearning for death. (The allusion to Wagner helps us to see that the god's "last desire" is, in fact, death.) Sometimes we give the word *theme* to an organizing principle that sorts out the details in a work, and sometimes we use other words. Unfortunately the vocabulary of literary criticism is very irregular. When the organizing principle can be visualized, I prefer to call it a superintendent image; when it is an idea or a feeling, I generally call it a motive.

An ordered reading does more than just copy the text in the mind however, for it also furnishes the text with details which the author has not presented explicitly but which belong there nevertheless because they are required for a total constituting. We make these additions so naturally and easily that we seldom realize that they are our own contributions, not the author's. Robinson, for instance, does not plainly say that his lines describe an imagined end of the world, but we add that interpretation rather confidently anyway. Some critics have gone so far as to claim that readers may understand a work better than the person who wrote it. And, indeed, sometimes, without realizing it, we contradict an author. Few readers of Shakespeare, for instance, conceive Hamlet to be thirty (a fact deducible from the first clown's speeches in V, i, 146–168) and overweight (V, ii, 287). Perhaps this example of Hamlet puts us right on the borderline between an ordered reading and the disorder when the student's meanings were substituted for those of Hopkins. If we want to read Shakespeare, we had better take Hamlet as Shakespeare presents him, and leave romanticizing his appearance to Ophelia; otherwise we are not so much constituting the play as mutilating it.

Finally, a good reading is abundant. It has to be in order to conform with the several dimensions of meaning in a work. Literary works possess several kinds of meaning. They can mean in the ordinary prosaic way of giving messages about the world ("Murder will out," "Beauty is Truth"). Or they can mean archetypally by awakening deep interpersonal associations ("Removing the weeds, putting fresh soil about the bean stems, and encouraging this weed which I had sown, making the yellow soil express its summer thought in bean leaves and blossoms rather than in wormwood and piper and millet grass, making the earth say beans instead of grass,—this was my daily work."[4]). Or they can mean as actions. For instance, it is the action that signifies everything when Caesar stops defending himself as soon as he sees that one of his attackers is Brutus. Works can also have meaning in a self-referential way, as when Hardy composes *The Mayor of Casterbridge* so that Henchard's career symmetrically goes from poor journeyman hay-trusser, gradually up to mayor, and then through equally gradual declinations back to hay-trusser again. Or self-reference may take such intricate forms in verse as the sestina, or it may go as far as shaped poems like George Herbert's "The Altar" or "Easter Wings," in which the form that the poem takes on the page alludes to the content.

Such a variety in the separate elements of meaning and in the kinds of meaning that fill a work requires prolonged and repeated mental activity to be actualized by the reader, and this is why serious reading of an important work stretches out over a long span, sometimes even years. We go back to works again and again, rereading the shorter ones many times in the effort of comprehension, in the case of longer works rehearsing them in our minds and frequently reviewing key passages and overall design.

Not just any response made for the sake of achieving abundance will do, of course, because a helter-skelter search for every possible personal connection with the work violates order. But within the limits which the work sets upon the consciousness, the reader hopes for enriched experience by discovering weighty masses of significance. According to Monroe C. Beardsley, the distinctive feature of literature as compared to other modes that employ words is the large place which literature gives to implication.[5] The remarkable concentration of meaning in literature—and hence a large part of its intensity—results from implication, which allows more thought and feeling to be compacted into far fewer words than ordinary discourse requires. This difference becomes readily noticeable if we compare two short passages, one unliterary and the other literary, and try to paraphrase them.

Here is a popular little verse, certainly amusing in its own way, which makes
no attempt at compression or, indeed, literary merit of any kind.

> We had a little Johnny.
> Now Johnny is no more;
> For what he thought was H_2O
> Was H_2SO_4.

"Our John drank sulfuric acid, mistaking it for water, and he died." This
rhymed joke succeeds very well as humor, but it is not a serious attempt
at literature, and the ease with which it leads to paraphrase shows that one
literary characteristic which it lacks is implication (all the meaning is on the
surface) and that another missing feature is concentration (the paraphrase is
shorter than the verse). By contrast, here is a stanza, only a little longer, of
a two-stanza poem called "Gemini" by the contemporary poet Richard
Wilbur.[6]

> Because poor PUER's both unsure and vain,
> Those who befriend him suffer his disdain,
> While those who snub him gain his deference.
> He loves his enemies in a certain sense.

Wilbur's verse, like the other, also has a comic intention, but clearly it is
more than a mere joke based on simple incongruity. Bits of meaning flicker
out, criss-cross the lines, and connect with other shreds of meaning in the
poem or with conventional associations in the reader's mind. PUER, the
Latin word for *boy*, stands midway between abstraction and specific characterization. The phrase "he loves his enemies" alludes to a memorable
sentence of Jesus' beginning "Love your enemies" (Matt. 5:44), and yet
Wilbur's qualifying phrase, "in a certain sense," implies that PUER's love
differs from the love that moral law dictates, that indeed it even perverts
and caricatures that love. PUER, we know, is both a snob and a toady. Still
the poem warns us not to go too far in our condemnation. He is "poor
PUER," and we remind ourselves, just in the nick of time perhaps, that if we
scorn him for being beneath us we shall have committed exactly the sin that,
in him, tempts us to despise him.

   An indication of an abundant reading is that it picks up as large a
number of signals in a text as can be ordered into a unified object of
contemplation. The two parts of this requirement do not easily coincide with
each other. On the one hand, we can concentrate so much attention on the
details of a richly meaningful work that we lose the sense of its form and it
becomes a mere pastiche of themes, figures of speech, images, and so on. On
the other hand, we can make up our minds too early about a work's meaning
or value or even about the experience it can provide us, and the result of our
haste may be that we ignore just the characteristics in the work that make it

uniquely wonderful. We ought to find the happy medium between the reading that deforms the work by falsely magnifying accidental details and the one which strips a work down to vacuous symbols. We have a better chance to succeed if we become dexterous in the double process of making up our minds and also of keeping our minds open to new perceptions at the same time. With practice we improve in this subtle operation.

Perhaps just here we come to a principal use of literature in forming the mind. A liberally educated person has a tact for provisional closure, for belief without bigotry. That tact is a valuable civility, one which the study of literature may help to inculcate.

5 Finding Adequate Methods

The first step in devising a teaching method is to determine the goal, or in other words, to answer the question, "Why should students learn this subject?" The grounds for reading literature are extremely various, running all the way from claims that literature provides vicarious experience, to arguments that it nurtures imagination—which may be the ultimate basis of reason—to the contention that it imparts ideas ineffable in ordinary discourse, to various escapist theories—like Shopenhauer's that says literature is a resource humans possess to guard their minds against the implacable and malevolent drift of a crazed world. Still other explanations of the value of literature exist. Strictly, though, these arguments assert the value of particular works, not of literature in general. Every endorsement of the value of literature assumes that it is the actual reading of single, separate works that is the good thing, not the digesting of works into our general fund of information, not even the growth in our skill to read more works. It is the particular poem or play or story that *is* good and *does* good; everything else is secondary.

This point of view is so radically different from the outlook governing the teaching of most other subjects that we have to grasp it very firmly in order not to swim with the tide and teach literature in the same way that our colleagues teach history and physics, for example, or that we ourselves, quite rightly, teach grammar and composition. It may be instructive to compare our works as teachers of literature to our work as teachers of the other fields of English. If we were able in one year to teach our students the four works that are dealt with in the next section of this book, and if we felt that those works had "found" those students, had moved them, had connected with their lives, surely the most ambitious of us would be thoroughly pleased, even exultant. We would not lament because the students had not read Milton or Wordsworth or other greats.

Not so with grammar. Suppose that we had a student who knew the noun to its depths—common nouns, proper nouns, abstract nouns, concrete nouns, infinitive and gerundival nouns—and suppose also that the student fully grasped the genitive, the case of pronouns, parallel structure, and the different kinds of subordinate clauses. Would we be satisfied? Indeed not, if the student did not also know verbs and all the other parts of speech, participles, negation, agreement, degrees of comparison, and so on, and on, and on.

It is the same with composition. A student who knows all about topic sentences and has a virtuoso ability to vary syntactic structures still fails importantly as a writer without also possessing the skill to use transitions or to find accurate words for expressing ideas. In grammar and composition, as in most formal academic disciplines, one can hardly be said to know anything valuable about a subject before learning a great deal about it. On the other hand, literature and the other arts present a very different case. Wordsworth's *Intimations Ode* and Beethoven's *Violin Concerto* are good things in themselves and by themselves, and the student who has come to possess either one of them has once and forever secured a substantial addition to his or her mental life. If the student adds to these acquirements Milton's "On the Morning of Christ's Nativity" or Tchaikovsky's *Violin Concerto,* so much the better, but these additions are not essential to his or her art life in the way that getting a complete view of the principles of grammar or of composition is essential to becoming a decent linguist or writer.

So it seems, then, that the literature teacher's goal for the students has to do with individual works and not with collections of works whether grouped according to genre, period, or theme. And with respect to those individual works, the teacher's goal is primarily to aid students to read them aesthetically, as literary works, just as the music teacher's goal is to get them to hear music aesthetically and the art teacher's goal is to get them to see paintings and sculptures aesthetically. To experience these things aesthetically is to experience them as event-object-meanings which fill up the whole consciousness and shape it in accordance with their own complex, intense being. To experience them unaesthetically is to trivialize them by taking them as incidental recreations (a few lines of verse to embellish a conversation or speech, music to give background to a dinner party, a print put on one side of a window to balance a lamp on the other side). Another way to experience them unaesthetically is to deprive them of their autonomy as objects and events in their own right and to subordinate them to something else, as the humanities teacher does who plans a unit on immigrants and tarts it up with a movement from the *New World Symphony,* a slice of pizza, and a shillelagh, all presented on the same level as illustrating the topic. Literature teachers know better than to misuse art so crudely, but even so, they are tempted now and then to reduce literary works to moral homilies: *Macbeth* is still sometimes used to caution students against ambition, and Browning's "Epilogue to *Asolando*" is occasionally employed to make them admire it.

We have already seen what an aesthetic response is; it is the pleasurable result that occurs when attention has been arrested, prolonged, and concluded by an event-object-meaning. Our job as teachers of literature is to make it possible for our students to read some few works so that their consciousness is dealt with in just that way. That operation is enormously complex, and, involving the many-sided relations among teacher, student, and work, it is unique in each case and there is no possibility whatever of putting it in a nutshell of a few dozen behavioral objectives, each beginning "the student will be able to . . ." and ending ". . . eighty-five percent of the tasks." But, on the other hand, we need not abandon ourselves to desperate trial-and-error methods either. Reason and experience take us at least a little way.

Points That Determine Methods

To begin with, we know that three main points of reference decide our methods. These points are: the character of the teacher, the character of the students, and the character of the work. The teacher has personal idiosyncrasies of taste and discernment, a natural affinity for one writer but not for another, for one genre or period and not another. Beyond that, the teacher's own scholarly training and personal program of reading give rise to special familiarity with certain fields. By all means the teacher should make use of these strengths in making teaching plans. If the teacher has taken a good course in Hawthorne but lacks knowledge of Melville, then *The Scarlet Letter* or *The House of Seven Gables* should be chosen over *Moby Dick* when the time comes to teach a nineteenth century American novel, or if the teacher reads Wordsworth with appreciation but cannot approach Shelley sympathetically, then obviously "The World Is Too Much with Us" should be chosen over "Ozymandias" when teaching a sonnet. We choose authors and works that we admire and understand because we can teach them much better than we can teach the others, a fact that may partly account for the popularity of high school electives among both teachers and students. True, a habit of teaching our own favorite works, especially if those works fail to match our students' interests and abilities, can lead to eccentricity and excess. Doubtless, for instance, the teacher who happens to be writing a dissertation on the novels of Captain Marryat or on insects in seventeenth century poetry may very well overestimate the students' tolerance for lectures on those subjects. But since a teacher can be placed on guard against those enthusiasms that students will not share, the benefits involved in teaching one's own field of strength are greater than the risks.

There is a serious danger of a somewhat different kind, however, if year after year the teacher goes on offering the same works. As mentioned earlier, literary study has an element of adventure for the reader, of discovering something new and of risking failure in the attempt at discovery. Once the teacher loses that sense of adventure, once the old familiar works lose their freshness and their mystery and serve merely as protection against the need to study new material, the teacher no longer presents a model to students for the adventurous aspect of reading literature. Such a teacher is no longer a dependable associate in an interesting enterprise, but is instead a technician managing students' reactions, approving some ideas, rejecting others, shushing the rebellious, assigning papers, enlightening the puzzled, and confounding the confident. Teachers in the movies may look good doing that, but that is no way to teach literature.

This problem of the teacher's getting into a rut as a consequence of incessantly teaching the same familiar works has a simple solution: It is for teachers to remain active in their own programs of reading literature. Teachers who keep on reading fine books throughout their professional lives will not only possess a gradually expanding set of works and the competency to teach them, but also their mastery of the old works will be deepened and strengthened. The teacher who regularly offers *Othello* to students, for instance, but who also keeps up independent reading may eventually come across Iris Murdoch's novel *Fairly Honourable Defeat,* where, in the character of the scientist Julius Klein, is to be found a twentieth century version of the Iago personality. It is an intriguing view of Iago's character, a view that emphasizes the childish malice, innocent as it were through emotional privation, which is to be found in adults who have not matured in their feelings about themselves or others.

The teacher may feel that other professional obligations must come before personal reading. Classes must be prepared carefully, there must be frequent conferences with students, at least some professional writing in English education ought to be read, and there are all the other duties, including the onerous burden of reading students' compositions. There is only one way of setting these distractions aside, and that is for the teacher to become personally convinced once and for all, that of all the professional functions, the one that must have priority is one's own program of reading literature. Perhaps the complaint about teachers that was often heard years ago and which still surfaces now and then—that they know how to teach but do not know what to teach—has no truth whatever. But true or false as a generalization, it indicates the reason why teachers of literature must individually put first their own continuing growth in their subject. Without that growth the teacher goes stale and loses zest for a field that is no longer cultivated— and teaching becomes a grind for teacher and students alike. No matter how sedulous such a teacher is in marking papers, conferring with students and parents, taking part in professional meetings and so on, he or she is nothing but a talented drudge, mechanically cranking out material that each year gets drier as the teacher becomes more removed from the immediate experience of reading it. The difference between the real teacher and the mere pedagogue is that the teacher has something to say which the students ought to hear.

Students and the Choice of Method

The second point of reference which we employ in deciding on methods—
the character of the students—can vary widely from one class to another even
for the same teacher, who will continually need to adjust the content and
means of instruction to different kinds of students. Perhaps the key word is
the character, not the intellectual quality, of the students, for the kind of
person that one is has far more bearing on the experience that is gained
from a literary work than does one's educational attainment or perhaps even
one's intelligence as standard tests determine it. By observation of students a
teacher can confirm the fact that in literary study depth of personality counts
as much as intellectual brilliance. It is by no means always the brightest
students, as usually defined, who see farthest into a literary work, and indeed
the unprompted comments of ordinary students on poems and stories that
fully engage them are virtually identical in thought with the insights of
professional scholars and critics.

If the student is to constitute a work richly, the teacher's help is needed.
To some extent, an ingenious teacher can offer readiness activities which will
heighten a student's powers of constituting in such ways as are recounted
by Edmund J. Farrell in his essay "Listen, My Children, and You Shall Read"[1]
or by James Herndon in his books *The Way It Spozed to Be* and *How to
Survive in Your Native Land*.[2] To a larger extent, the teacher can adapt the
curriculum in literature to the students' development. Selecting the works
for teaching with an eye to the requirements of our students does not mean
that we are lowering our standards; rather it reflects our knowledge that
people at different stages in their lives are more fitted for some art
experiences than for others. Generally, high school teachers have dropped
Silas Marner from the curriculum because they realize that this magnificent
book, surpassing the emotional development of most of their students,
necessarily seems dull to them. On the other hand, *The Scarlet Letter* and
Moby Dick remain in the curriculum, for although they are intrinsically quite
as difficult as *Silas Marner,* their difficulties are of another kind and within
the young adult's power to master.

Methods in Relation to Subject

Finally, the nature of our subject, literature, has much to do with the methods
that we select. In the first place, the literary experience, involving as it does
both the constituting of the work and also the special aesthetic contemplation
of that work, is so different from the sort of experience habitual with
students that they will need the teacher's help if they are to attain it at
all. The teacher will choose activities that focus students' attention on the

relevant and the important aspects of literature, not the pointless and trivial. In our daily lives, governed more by necessity than choice, it may be relevant to know that the principal is a stuffed shirt; but in reading *The Portrait of a Lady,* it is unnecessary to decide about Henry James's personality. In the student's daily life it is important, or at least interesting, to be able to surmise that a teacher quarreled with her husband last night; but it is merely distracting to ask the question whether Lady Macbeth had been married before she became Macbeth's wife. The student learns to discriminate between aesthetic experience that is banal and that which is rich according to the questions, projects, and information that the teacher offers, and the student who has the luck to get a superior teacher will perceive that reading literature is even a finer thing than talking about it.

In addition to helping the student to make a reading that is aesthetic, the teacher must also provide for a reading that specifically answers to the particular work. Shelley's "Skylark" and Hopkins's "Windhover" express perfervid urgency; Wordsworth's "Ode to Duty" and Gray's "Elegy Written in a Country Churchyard" convey a calmer spirit of detached meditation. The student, having never read the poems before, knows nothing about their feeling-tone, and therefore has no clue as to how to address them. Here the teacher can help, both with the information that is given and also, more subtly, with the appropriate methods. The discursiveness of the poems by Wordsworth and Gray permits a larger amount of lecture and free-ranging discussion than do "Skylark" and "Windhover," which will more fully open themselves to a different kind of teaching—to reading aloud, for instance— and to convergent questioning. The effective teacher of literature first studies the text to determine what range of experience that text ought to produce in a sympathetic reader, and then draws on a repertoire of teaching practices for just the methods that will help the students to entertain the appropriate experience.

To summarize the conclusions that we have reached so far: (1) the right goal for students is to know individual works aesthetically, in themselves; (2) the methods selected by the teacher in order to reach this goal are conditioned by three factors—the teacher, the students, and the work. Now, perhaps, we are ready to consider the question of methods in more detail.

The Two Dimensions of Literature

Since literary works exist along two separate but related dimensions, the reader must attend to both. The one dimension consists of the individual parts: the single line (fast or slow, flowing or interrupted, euphonious or harsh), the single image (clear or misty, complete or fragmentary, opulent or spare), the single word (formal or informal, connotative or denotative, explicit or equivocal). This dimension we can call *the text,* and the reader's knowledge of it we can call *textual awareness* or, to express the particularity that is involved in this kind of knowledge, *micro-awareness.* The other dimension exists in the relation of these parts to each other (the way one word modifies another word or image, the congruence or conflict between figures of speech) and also in the total arrangement of all the parts into an intelligible pattern (the birth-harvest-death pattern of "To Autumn," the summer-fall-winter-spring pattern of *Walden*). This dimension might be called *the form,* and the reader's knowledge of this aspect of the work we can call *formal awareness* or, to indicate the omnifaceted totality of this knowing, *macro-awareness.*

Fortunately, the most effective way to teach micro-awareness is also an easy way; it is simply to read the text aloud. This reading aloud almost immediately gives the student a number of impressions that can be welded together as the work is being constituted. One set of impressions is rhythmic. From hearing the work read correctly the student senses the pattern of its meter and the larger flow of melody that embraces, modifies, enlarges that pattern, and counterpoints it. Here is Shakespeare writing iambic pentameter lines in Sonnet 60.

> Like as the waves make towards the pebbled shore,
> So do our minutes hasten to their end,

It would be a pity if a student who knows only that iambic meter alternates a weak and a loud stress were left alone to constitute these lines and so belted them out like this:

> Like AS the WAVES make TOWARDS the PEBBled SHORE,
> So DO our MINutes HASTen TO their END,

The student would miss entirely the better reading that both imitates the slow, calm but fierce, surge of ocean waves and also hints at the inevitability of growing older.

> LIKE as the WAVES / / máke towards the pébbled SHORE,
> SO do our MINutes / / hásten to their END,

A sense of pitch can be added to the impressions of rhythm. Here, for instance, is an iambic pentameter line from Pope's "Epistle to Dr. Arbuthnot," where there is both a distinctive melody and a distinctive pitch.

> Now trips a Lady, and now struts a Lord.
> (Nów trips a Lády, / / and NOW STRUTS a LORD.)

The first half of the line quick and mincing with frontal and high-pitched vowels, the second half swaggering and slow with heavy back vowels—this eighteenth century Bronx cheer maliciously heckles Pope's enemy, Lord Hervey.

The rhythmic and tonal qualities of a work affect its meaning, often providing speech cadences that substantially modify a propositional statement. Thus, Thoreau begins *Walden* in the pure Yankee guise: He spits out a paralleled series of factual statements; there is no warmth of feeling, no pretense of familiarity. He and his reader stay on opposite sides of a fence constructed of exact statements that give away nothing but the literal event, and the personalities on both sides remain guarded, self-sufficient.

> When I wrote the following pages, or rather the bulk of them, I lived alone, in the woods, a mile from any neighbor, in a house which I had built myself, on the shore of Walden Pond, in Concord, Massachusetts, and earned my living by the labor of my hands only. I lived there two years and two months. At present I am a sojourner in civilized life again.

One can write a few paragraphs in that spirit, but hardly a book, and soon—though not immediately—Thoreau allows us a nearer approach. By Chapter XIV, "Winter Visitors," he and his readers are so familiar that he is willing to risk this final paragraph in the chapter, a paragraph that, read aloud, reveals in its rhythms a great openness and even a painful vulnerability.

> There too, as everywhere, I sometimes expected the Visitor who never comes. The Vishnu Purana says, "The house-holder is to remain at eventide in his court-yard as long as it takes to milk a cow, or longer if he pleases, to await the arrival of a guest." I often performed this duty of hospitality, waited long enough to milk a whole herd of cows, but did not see the man approaching from the town.

When Thoreau wrote the opening paragraph of *Walden*, he was not willing that we should see such spiritual yearning in himself as he reveals here, but now he is on close terms with us. The crisp, angry inflection of the phrase "waited long enough to milk a whole herd of cows" is not directed at us; rather it expresses our exasperation as much as Thoreau's against "the Visitor who never comes."

Doubtless the elucidations that I have just tried to make by referring to the rhythms and sounds in the texts are inadequate and even misleading. That is exactly the point. In a good literary work the process of qualification and specification of meaning is so extremely complex that no merely critical analysis can possibly keep pace with it. If I were to attempt to say all that Shakespeare, Pope, and Thoreau have said in the passages just quoted, then I should have to write a literary work myself and not just commentary. But although teachers cannot hope to articulate in words the whole range of a work's significations, they can let the work speak for itself merely by having it read aloud. To a very large extent, works can explain themselves, and we best serve both the works and our students by exposing them to each other and then quickly getting out of the way.

Perhaps an example out of my own teaching will make this point. Once I attempted to teach Faulkner's short novel "Spotted Horses" to a college Freshman English class. It was a recitation class based mainly on congruent questions calling for short, factual answers. These answers showed that the students had read the story, rather closely indeed, but also that they had simply not realized that it is funny. Not knowing what else to do, I read some of my favorite passages: Henry Armstid's trying to take his pony out of the corral and getting his arm broken, the landlady's smashing a washboard over the head of a confused horse that has invaded her house, the Texan's wrestling a horse to the ground as he alternately swears at it and extols its merits to the bidders at the auction. Soon we were all laughing.

Who is best suited to read aloud? In most instances, I should say the teacher. True, some writers read their own works exceptionally well, but a number do not. As for professional actors, they can certainly present drama better than most teachers can, but as I discovered when trying to find phonograph recordings for the teaching units in the next section, their rendition of other genres of literature often is more mellifluous than insightful. One famous actor's reading of the first line of Keats's "To Autumn"—"Season of mists and mellow fruitfulness,"—raps it out in a loud, fast, joyful declamation, which is surely false to the poem. A teacher, teaching works that are known intimately from having lived with them, will rarely make such a mistake. In spite of that strength, we teachers sometimes hesitate and ask recorded actors to do something that we can do better ourselves. Perhaps because literature gives striking form to feelings that we are reluctant to confess publicly, perhaps because it calls for a vocal beauty we lack, many of us feel embarrassed to read aloud to our classes, and so we hurry over the reading or avoid it altogether. In such cases we should acknowledge that we are in the wrong and start to form right habits.

The following few points may help the teacher to get up nerve, beginning with the realization that however faulty the teacher's own reading of a familiar work may appear to be, it is almost certainly better than the students'. The reading can be rehearsed as a part of the teacher's preparation for the class, and a tape recorder can be used to build confidence by listening to the performance in advance. Finally, realizing that reading aloud can become one of the teacher's chief distinctions, it can be deliberately cultivated through practice or even through speech courses which are available as a part of professional preparation.

But should not the students be encouraged to read aloud? Well, certainly there are educational advantages to them in doing so. Those advantages include a chance to engage more deeply with the work or passage and to benefit by fully sensing its tonal and rhythmic qualities. Students will stand to learn more, however, if their reading has been modelled on the teacher's more accomplished performance (not necessarily of the same works, of course). For that reason alone there should be plenty of reading by the teacher. In addition, it simply is not fair to ask a student to read without any advance notice and preparation, for no one can read a work decently without some practice. A means of using the oral reading of students to increase their familiarity with a work or a passage is to ask a number of them to prepare readings of it that differ with respect to speed and stress. For instance, two students can prepare two different readings, one very fast, one slow, of the opening lines of Hopkins's "Windhover":

> I caught this morning morning's minion, king-
> > dom of daylight's dauphin, dapple-dawn-drawn Falcon, in his riding
> > Of the rolling level underneath him steady air, and striding
> High there, how he rung upon the rein of a wimpling wing
> In his ecstasy!

Another two students can give a fast reading and a slow reading of the opening lines of Hopkins's "Spring and Fall":

> Márgarét, áre you gríeving
> Over Goldengrove unleaving?
> Léaves, líke the things of man, you
> With your fresh thoughts care for, can you?

Another way of focusing students' attention on the details of a work is by *explication de texte*. This phrase has two meanings. One meaning, associated with the school of New Criticism, refers to a strategy for elucidating a work by closely scrutinizing its structure. The other, older, meaning is the sense in which the term is intended here. Originally, *explication de texte* was a French schoolroom exercise used in teaching literature, especially poetry. In that exercise, the student was given a very few lines, two or three perhaps, and then was required to state all the information that would activate the meaning and the beauty of those lines. In short, *explication de texte* in this second sense is an exercise in constituting.

Here is how the exercise can operate to aid students' micro-awareness. The teacher gives the students a short poem or a stanza either by writing it on the blackboard or by handing it out in ditto sheets. The poem is read. Then the teacher calls on each person in the class, the teacher included, to make one brief statement about any aspect of the poem which happens to be of interest. Only two rules apply: (1) no one is to offer a statement that is believed to be silly, (2) but neither should anyone hold back a statement out of fear that others might think it trivial or pointless. Repetitions are likely and need not be avoided. After everyone has commented at least once, the teacher can ask what other statements ought to be made, and these can be collected randomly as the students offer them. I have used for this exercise the following poem by Thomas Hardy.

> The Fallow Deer at the Lonely House
>
> One without looks in to-night
>   Through the curtain-chink
> From the sheet of glistening white;
> One without looks in to-night
>   As we sit and think
>   By the fender-brink.
>
> We do not discern those eyes
>   Watching in the snow;
> Lit by lamps of rosy dyes
> We do not discern those eyes
>   Wondering, aglow,
>   Fourfooted, tiptoe.

I have given this poem to ninth grade students, college seniors, and graduate students, and the responses have been similar at all three levels. The three levels also are alike in their omissions: Whenever I have given the poem I have had to supply items #1 and #7, listed below. Other than those two exceptions, almost any class can provide the following statements.

1. A "fallow deer" is the European deer, like the North American animal but somewhat smaller.
2. The word *one* is intermediate between *someone* and *something*. This deer is not quite a person, but it is not just an animal either, as we usually think of animals.
3. The coziness of indoors contrasts with the cold of outdoors.
4. The colorfulness of indoors contrasts with the blank white of outdoors.
5. Yet the deer, outdoors, has a spot of color in its eyes.
6. The poem gives no hint of the deer's sex, but one is inclined to think of it as female.
7. "Fender-brink" refers to the guard-rail around a fireplace or stove.
8. It is a fireplace, not a stove.
9. The poem emphasizes the difference in character between the humans and the deer.
10. Perhaps the deer is cold.
11. It may be that the deer wants to come in.
12. On the other hand, the deer may be merely curious about the insiders.

13. From one viewpoint, this poem describes a zoo, with the relations of animals and humans reversed.

14. It is the deer's eyes, not the humans', that are "lit by lamps of rosy dyes."

15. The "rosy dyes" are the reflections of the light from the open fireplace in the deer's eyes.

16. Ungulates like the deer (and horses and cows) have large, dark pupils in their eyes which reflect light and serve as prisms to break it into many colors.

17. It may be that the deer's eyes, reflecting and refracting the firelight, are the lamps which light "us" inside the room.

18. It is the deer's *eyes* that are described as "wondering, aglow, / Fourfooted, tiptoe." The parallel structure indicates that.

19. The eyes are fourfooted in the sense that the deer is a dumb animal, unable to express its feelings and perhaps even unable to know its feelings.

20. Probably humans know their own feelings better than other animals do, but we cannot be sure.

21. The eyes are tiptoe in two senses: (a) the deer, an ungulate, walks literally on tiptoe, on its toenails; (b) this deer is tiptoe with excited curiosity.

22. The humans are not certain that there is a deer outside.

23. They *hope* there is a deer at the window. They *think* there may be one.

24. The poem combines cold and warmth.

25. The poem also combines privation and ease.

26. The deer yearns toward the humans; the humans yearn toward the deer.

27. The outdoors and the inside of the house are distinct but not absolutely divorced. The curtain-chink, the deer's bright eyes, and the humans' imaginations slightly connect inside and outside.

28. Inside is a company of people, or at least a couple; outside is the solitary deer.

29. Humans sit and think; the other animals stand and watch.

30. Humans and the other higher animals have much in common, are interested in each other, but also they are too different to have a mutual understanding.

31. The deer is full of excited interest; the humans are relaxed and easy.

32. It may be that the humans inside the house understand each other no better than they understand the deer outside.

33. The deer may be just as content as the humans. She may not feel uncomfortably cold.

34. But she may. We cannot know.

35. It is not totally dark outside even though it is night-time. The snow is "glistening white."

36. The poem describes beings who are by necessity separated but who would like to know each other.

37. The poem is both happy and sad.

Macro-awareness results when the reader's consciousness conforms to the event-object-meaning which makes up the whole work. Such intense awareness is obviously difficult to achieve, and we have to go back to a work often before we really do achieve it. One way that a teacher can help students to hold a complete work in their minds is to assist them in comparing and contrasting it with other works in a different medium that elicit similar responses. A well-illustrated book performs just that function. In the teaching unit on Keats's "To Autumn," I have suggested some landscapes with which the poem can be compared and contrasted according to their different effects, and I have suggested another nature poem, Riley's "When the Frost Is on the Pun'kin," which contrasts with Keats's poem in a way to emphasize some of its distinctive features. Teachers can use bulletin boards effectively for this purpose, and many teachers, after some years of service, have collected magnificent sets of pictures which, though referred to as "ephemeral material" in methods texts, are anything but ephemeral in their effect on students' minds.

Another way of helping students to attend to the whole work closely is, when near the beginning of a unit, to ask questions that apply to the complete structure and then to bring up those questions now and again in the discussion of particular reading assignments. Thus, in dealing with a lengthy novel such as *Moby Dick* we can ask more than once the question, "With which of the characters do you feel the most sympathy and with which the most antipathy?" and, depending on the section being discussed, the answer will change from time to time until the novel is finished.

A different way of drawing attention to the wholeness of works is to use plot diagrams. Many dramas and some novels are organized on this structural basis:[3]

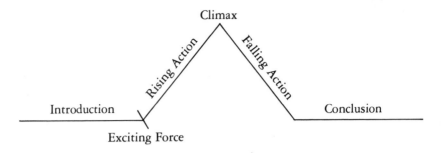

Other plots can be represented by different diagrams. The plot of Willa Cather's *The Professor's House* might be shown in this way:

Main Action	Inserted Episode	Main Action

The main action gets its focus in an episode that took place years earlier and in a man who, though dead, remains the principal actor in affecting the fortunes of the others.

Another way of helping students clarify their whole view of the complete work is to invite them to see it for a moment from some outlook radically different from their own. As meanings, fine works are almost inevitably ambiguous; they point to different conclusions that are not entirely consistent with each other. Thus, although we read *Hamlet* in a way that is sympathetic to the hero's standpoint, once we step away from it a little we see that he has human faults that help to make him the man that he is. If a student were asked to give a short talk on the question "Who would make the better king, Claudius or Hamlet?" the student, as well as the others in the class, would probably be surprised by insights into Hamlet's character that would not otherwise have been discovered. Another instance of ambiguity in the meaning of a work is Keats's *Lamia.* At one point in that poem Keats asks which of the three main characters we should pity and gives this answer to his own question:

> What wreath for Lamia? What for Lycius?
> What for the sage, old Apollonius?
> Upon her aching forehead be there hung
> The leaves of willow and of adder's tongue;
> And for the youth, quick, let us strip for him
> The thyrsus, that his watching eyes may swim
> Into forgetfulness; and, for the sage,
> Let spear-grass and the spiteful thistle wage
> War on his temples.

> (Part II, lines 221–229)

These lines suggest that Keats himself gave most of his sympathy to young

Lycius, the searcher for an impossible beauty in this world; that he pitied Lamia, the incarnation of mysterious charm; and that he scorned the rationalist scholar Apollonius, who with his realism destroyed the other two. Yet, as commentators have noticed, this poem also hints at other, very different, views of the characters, suggesting that Apollonius is the only one of the three who, being honest, is also really loving, and that Lamia and Lycius are, respectively, a fraud and a gullible weakling.

Walt Whitman normally does not strike us as an ambiguous poet. Yet the poem below (Number 11 in "Song of Myself") sets off in us two contrary feelings—first a conventional stereotype and, a little later, a humane antidote to that stereotype:

> Twenty-eight young men bathe by the shore,
> Twenty-eight young men and all so friendly;
> Twenty-eight years of womanly life and all so lonesome.
>
> She owns the fine house by the rise of the bank,
> She hides handsome and richly dressed aft the blinds of
> the window.
>
> Which of the young men does she like the best?
> Ah the homeliest of them is beautiful to her.
>
> Where are you off to, lady? for I see you,
> You splash in the water there, yet stay stock still in
> your room.
>
> Dancing and laughing along the beach came the twenty-ninth
> bather,
> The rest did not see her, but she saw them and loved them.
>
> The beards of the young men glisten'd with wet, it ran
> from their long hair,
> Little streams pass'd all over their bodies.
>
> An unseen hand also pass'd over their bodies,
> It descended tremblingly from their temples and ribs.
>
> The young men float on their backs, their white bellies
> bulge to the sun, they do not ask who seizes fast to them,
> They do not know who puffs and declines with pendant and
> bending arch,
> They do not think whom they souse with spray.

At first we despise the spinster who peeps through her window blinds at the naked men bathing in the sea. For us she is the conventional old maid, superficially a prude but secretly a libidinal furnace. The poem soon subverts that bigotry, however, and it leads us to sympathize and even in some degree to admire her. She possesses a "womanly life," is "handsome," and is called "lady." And when in her dream of bliss she comes "Dancing and laughing along the beach," we feel ourselves to be on her side, for we know that her frustrated life is in a measure redeemed by the boisterous normality of her fantasy. If in the first stanza we admire the men and condemn the woman, long before the end of the poem those feelings are turned around so that we lose patience with the dullards who have no sense of their hidden lover. In this poem the neurotic old maid has seen; the healthy young men have not seen.

Finally, students can be helped to see works whole if, after reading and discussing the works once, they come back to them again later for rereading, more discussion, and reconsideration. The spiral curriculum is adapted to no subject better than it is to the reading of literature, for we need to make many complex adjustments of sensibility in order at last to constitute an important work significantly. A proof that we need all the time we can use to understand fine works is that no teacher worth the salary would claim that, having read *Macbeth* before, it need not be studied again in order to teach it well. We spend all our lives reading certain poems, novels, and plays. By allowing students to go back to works for rereading and reconsideration, we not only help them to bring those works fully into consciousness, but we also develop in them the habits that will permit them to study literature by themselves in the way that it deserves to be studied.

Returning to shorter works is natural and easy. The teacher who understands students will know that reconsidering a lyric or short story will be profitable. Rereading longer works is more troublesome. If we give to them in the first encounter the careful attention which they merit, we shall not be likely in the same year to want to come back to them again for a vital reading. Yet many long works can be fruitfully reread over a person's secondary and college years, and each reading can draw from earlier ones and surpass them. *Walden, Huckleberry Finn,* and Arthurian romance all speak to every level of maturity, and students who read these works in junior high school, in high school, and again in college have done no more than begin an acquaintance which can profitably go on for a lifetime. Although a thorough rereading in class of a large number of long works is hardly feasible, those works need not be totally ignored after they have been taught. Simply giving continuity to the reading of literary works is a kind of spiraling. If an English class has read a selection of Shakespeare's sonnets and then goes on to read Milton's "On His Blindness," surely the teacher ought to ask the students if they notice differences of form in the two writers' work. Such a question can be enough to keep Shakespeare fresh in the students' minds.

Up to this point we have dealt with the teaching of works, and we have ignored the matter of teaching *about* works. There is a difference. When we ask students to find a word that most accurately describes the feeling-tone of Pope's *Essay on Man* we are teaching the work; when we tell them that this poem is neoclassical we are teaching *about* the work. If we help students find two lines in a passage from this poem that have different patterns of stress, we are teaching the work; if we lecture on the heroic couplet, we are teaching *about* the work. Teaching the work increases the students' consciousness of the particular piece of literature they are reading; teaching *about* the work imparts general literary or historical information which may be true and which may relate to the work but which does not cause that work to be the distinctive object that it is. Literary artists have a large resource of public information, belief, and practice which they use when they compose their works, but major artists will take material from this general, shared fund and then put it together in a way that is distinctive of just that particular thing that they make when they write one work or another.

How much teaching about works do students need in order to read literature as well as they can? The answer to this question is complex, and it must vary from one situation to another according to the many different combinations that are possible of students, teachers, and works. A seventh grade class reading in *The Song of Roland* Oliver's colorful description of the advancing Saracen army does not need much lecturing on medieval history or metrical romance, but a graduate seminar on the same poem can use all that information and more. Even though the specific amount of information which ought to be given will change, one principle remains constant. That principle is that, barring pedants and dilettantes, readers value the works more than they value information about the works. As a consequence, thoughtful teachers will confine themselves just to that ancillary information which they think will light up the works for their students. Furthermore, they will not subordinate the reading of a literary work to the study of psychiatry or the inculcation of a Marxist (or other) view of history or the memorization of figures of speech.

As was shown in Chapter III, all kinds of information can now and again help us to read works well. The teacher who remembers that this information is only for use in illuminating works will have a rule of thumb to serve as a guide in deciding how much of it to teach in any particular situation. All teachers need to remind themselves now and then that they are subject to intellectual vanity. Thus, we may get into a habit of thinking that no one can possibly read literature who is ignorant of similes and quatrains, but we shall be less exigent about prosopopoeia and prolepsis if we happen not to be familiar with those terms ourselves.[4]

Part II

6 Teaching the Lyric: Keats's "To Autumn"

To Autumn

Season of mists and mellow fruitfulness!
   Close bosom-friend of the maturing sun;
Conspiring with him how to load and bless
   With fruit the vines that round the thatch-eaves run;
To bend with apples the moss'd cottage-trees,
   And fill all fruit with ripeness to the core;
      To swell the gourd, and plump the hazel shells
   With a sweet kernel; to set budding more,
And still more, later flowers for the bees,
Until they think warm days will never cease,
   For Summer has o'er-brimm'd their clammy cells.

Who hath not seen thee oft amid thy store?
   Sometimes whoever seeks abroad may find
Thee sitting careless on a granary floor,
   Thy hair soft-lifted by the winnowing wind,
Or on a half-reap'd furrow sound asleep,
   Drowsed with the fume of poppies, while thy hook
      Spares the next swath and all its twinèd flowers;
And sometimes like a gleaner thou dost keep
   Steady thy laden head across a brook;
   Or by a cider-press, with patient look,
      Thou watchest the last oozings hours by hours.

Where are the songs of Spring? Ay, where are they?
   Think not of them, thou hast thy music too,—
While barrèd clouds bloom the soft-dying day,
   And touch the stubble-plains with rosy hue;
Then in a wailful choir the small gnats mourn
   Among the river sallows, borne aloft
      Or sinking as the light wind lives or dies;
And full-grown lambs loud bleat from hilly bourn;
   Hedge-crickets sing; and now with treble soft
   The red breast whistles from a garden-croft;
      And gathering swallows twitter in the skies.

Ideas and Images

The extraordinary richness of "To Autumn" invites imaginative speculation, and just to keep our bearings requires that we hold on to those characteristics of the poem which, though obvious, are also fairly certain. One plain characteristic is the principle of organization, which is an ordering of the details according to both the progress of the season and the progress of the day. Thus the season in the poem advances, from the ripening in the first stanza, to the harvesting in the second, and to the late autumn migration in the third. In addition, the poem follows the course of the day, from the morning mists of the first stanza on to the images of drowsy relaxation suggesting midday heat in the second stanza, and finally to the sunset and the swarming evening gnats of the last.

Another evident characteristic is the working of two different impulses. One of these impulses, the note of abundant generation, is prominent in the first stanza with its myriad fruit, flowers, and bees. The other impulse, the suggestion of decay and death, informs the last stanza, where it appears in the "soft-dying day," in the "wailful choir" of mourning gnats, in the crickets (which Keats thought replaced in winter the summer's grass-hopper),[1] and in the robins and swallows gathering for the annual migration. These two impulses, one at either end of the poem, appear to be linked to each other in the second stanza by the harvesting, a conventional symbol of abundance and of death.

A last certain point is that, for the form of this poem, Keats went back to the pattern of ode which he devised in the spring of 1819. "To Autumn" has the same tightly complex stanzaic construction, the same inherent ambivalence, and the same elaborate development of a presiding image as the earlier odes. The overall effect which these means generate is the feeling of opulence and density, an effect that is perhaps even stronger here than it is in the earlier works.

At first glance one would say that the presiding image of this poem is an autumn day, but that is only an approximate identification. The images derive not only from the day and the season, but they also originate in a personification which suffuses the poem. We can distinguish the presiding image more precisely by examining the first four lines.

> Season of mists and mellow fruitfulness!
>   Close bosom-friend of the maturing sun;
> Conspiring with him how to load and bless
>   With fruit the vines that round the thatch-eaves run.

The archetype of that image, which lay deep in Keats's mind, is sexual and familial love.[2] Here the image expands to vast dimensions. The lines concern cosmic love-making, with the feminine autumnal earth the "close bosom-friend" of the masculine "maturing sun," which in the fall begins to hover close to the earth and seems to lie upon it.[3] Their loving intercourse produces the rich fruitfulness which the first stanza details: apples, gourds, hazel nuts, flowers, bees, honey. Their mutual love extends to their offspring, whom they "conspire"[4] to make abound and flourish. These products of the earth and sun live in the warm, comfortable glow of the cosmic love that sustains them.

The second stanza, filled with scenes of harvesting, shows only the maternal figure, who serenely broods over her teeming produce. In the third stanza, however, which describes the late autumn decline of nature, the two figures of masculine sun and feminine earth come together once again. The splendid lines that celebrate their union are euphonious, picturesque, and suggestive:

> While barred clouds bloom the soft-dying day,
> And touch the stubble-plains with rosy hue;

The warm light of the setting sun, reflected from the cirrus clouds onto the autumnal earth, fondles it and their dying offspring in a loving embrace which now encompasses the death of things as earlier it had their germination. The music of autumn is a requiem, not a dirge; it is a meek and confident surrender to love.

J. M. Murry was right, I think, in saying that the meaning of "To Autumn" is expressed in Shakespeare's phrase "ripeness is all";[5] at least that interpretation is as nearly true to Keats's poem as a single assertion can be to an intricate whole work. Perhaps some further exploration will suggest those qualifications and additions that will make it truer still. The theme of cosmic benevolence is the main subject of this poem, and the image of that benevolence, the intercourse of sun and earth, presides serenely and lovingly over the death of things as well as their birth. The theme of benevolence in the universe is primarily a philosophic conception here, and consequently the death impulse in "To Autumn" is not the Freudian "death instinct," the movement toward destruction, negation, and extreme aggression. Instead, the death impulse in this poem is a conscious recognition that we must all die, and beyond that, a sober intuition that the infinite possibilities that we find within ourselves, or imagine that we find, are nonetheless limited by earthly conditions of life. Keats dwelt upon this idea at some length in the Vale of Soul-Making letter to George and Georgiana. Here is a part of the relevant passage:

> Look at the Poles and at the Sands of Africa, Whirlpools and volcanoes—
> Let men exterminate them and I will say that they may arrive at earthly happiness—The point at which Man may arrive is as far as the paralel [sic] state in inanimate nature and no further—For instance suppose a

rose to have sensation, it blooms on a beautiful morning it enjoys
itself—but there comes a cold wind, a hot sun—it cannot escape it, it
cannot destroy its annoyances—they are as native to the world as itself:
no more can man be happy in spite, the world[l]y elements will prey upon
his nature.[6]

Then in the letter Keats goes on to consider the question of how those
"worldly elements" can be used profitably, and his answer is that they are a
school in passing through which mere intelligence is educated into a
self-sufficient soul.

Although "To Autumn" does not follow the letter in asking what is the use
of earthly limitations in a man's life, still it does follow it in saying that those
limitations are good and not evil. The poem suggests that behind the
limitations, indeed within them, operates a complete system of sustaining
love. The ethic of the poem, that ripeness is all, is grounded in a metaphysics of a love that moves the sun and the other stars.

"To Autumn" is a major achievement in its own right, and it is
additionally interesting as the culmination of Keats's artistic development.
Considered in itself, "To Autumn" completely integrates the grand matter
and the grand manner, a great subject with commensurate treatment.
Considered as Keats's maturest poem, it happily reconciles two different
aspects of his genius—his intense concern with ideas and his sensuous delight
in physical things. In this respect, it strikes the reader as the mark toward
which Keats's artistic effort had been tending all along, the prototypical
Keatsian poem.

Keats himself consciously desired to unify his interest in things with his
interest in ideas, and the manner in which he effects that unification here
needs to be considered. He begins with things themselves—earth, sun, fruit,
and flowers—not with ideas of things. The reader of this poem feels not
that the earth *stands* for indulgence but rather that it *is* indulgent. For "To
Autumn" is neither an allegory nor an analogy; it is a perception, and its
figures are not emblems but true symbols, illustrations of a whole wide
system which they themselves partly constitute.

Thus the actions which the first stanza attributes to the sun and earth—
ripening, enlarging, unfolding—are factual deeds as well as metaphorical
expressions of cosmic solicitude. The figures of the second stanza grow so
naturally out of the real scene as to elude the artifice of personification.
The flow of chaff in the wind becomes the bright hair of a calm, half-reclining
woman, the eternal-mother, who emerges repeatedly in the stanza through
other heavily somnolent images. These data give us something seen, not
thought, the idea of an awful dignity in procreation.

"To Autumn" is crowded with process, with the vital on-goingness of all
being. Process is not the subject, however; instead it is the note of exuberant

reality which fills the poem and which is Keats's real interest. In this ode, as in the world, process signals reality, the energy of actual being. Just in this regard, "To Autumn" differs significantly from the other great odes, "Psyche," "Nightingale," and "Grecian Urn." Each of the earlier poems ostentatiously sets aside an area in which no process occurs: the eternal goddess safely abiding in the mind, the changeless nightingale singing its immortal song in the "passing night," the urn remaining through generations unscathed. The goddess, the nightingale, and the urn are changeless because they are not real, not actual beings. They are only ideas of things and not complete things themselves. "To Autumn," on the other hand, fills every part of its world with actual being and leaves no space for incomplete reality.

The effect of this difference in the metaphysics of "To Autumn" and the preceding odes is that whereas the earlier poems equivocally express a tension between ideas and things, "To Autumn" discovers a world of total reality. The earlier poems oppose ideas and things; "To Autumn" derives ideas from things. It shows all life as one vital existence and that existence as excellent and lovable.

Teaching the Poem

The Teacher's Preparation

A fine bibliography of scholarship on Keats, fully treated as well as carefully annotated, is Clarence D. Thorpe's chapter, now revised by David Perkins, in *The English Romantic Poets: A Review of Research and Criticism*, ed. Frank Jordan, Jr., 3rd ed. (New York: The Modern Language Association, 1972), pp. 379–448. A short, comprehensive, and beautifully written survey is Douglas Bush's *John Keats: His Life and Writings* (London: Weidenfeld and Nicolson, 1966) in the Masters of World Literature series. A longer and more detailed life, combined with sensitive critical commentary, is Walter Jackson Bate's *John Keats* (Cambridge, Mass.: Belknap Press, 1963). If the teacher plans to include "To Autumn" in a unit with other odes of Keats's, two good collections of essays can be found in G. S. Fraser, ed., *John Keats: Odes* (London: Macmillan, 1971) and in Jack Stillinger, ed., *Keats's Odes: A Collection of Essays* (Englewood Cliffs, N.J.: Prentice-Hall, 1968). Fraser's collection reprints Leonard Unger's splendid essay on "To Autumn," "Keats and the Music of Autumn"; Stillinger's essay summarizes it. Finally, an interesting "alternative interpretation" as she calls it is Annabel M. Patterson's "'How to load and . . . bend': Syntax and Interpretation in Keats's *To Autumn*," *PMLA*, 94 (March 1978), 449–457, in which she emphasizes the threatening, sinister motives in the poem.

Assignment

Like Keats's mature work generally, "To Autumn" has a surface simplicity masking profound depths of complicated feeling. Therefore, in order to read the poem successfully, the student will need plenty of time and plenty of help, and the help can begin right with the assignment. The study of "To Autumn" should begin with preliminary readiness work; a full period can be profitably employed. The teacher may want to introduce the poem by showing a picture or two of the countryside about Winchester which "To Autumn" describes, or by reading the passage from Keats's letter to his friend J. H. Reynolds in which he refers to the fine weather's suggesting the poem to him.[7] As part of the assignment the teacher should read the poem or else play a recording of it. (Neither of the two recordings of it that I have heard is very good.) The teacher should ask the students to note unfamiliar expressions (such as *clammy*) during the reading so that they can be explained at once. In addition, the assignment period is the right time for the teacher to describe the threshing process in the second stanza which suggests the image of a young woman

> . . . sitting careless on a granary floor,
> Thy hair soft-lifted by the winnowing wind.

In Keats's day, as in ages past, the entire grain plants—stalks, heads, and all—were laid out on a barn floor and then beaten with heavy wood flails so as to dislodge the kernels from the rest. Then, in the process called winnowing, the whole mass was put into a blanket and tossed up and down in the open air so that the chaff—straw, in our sense—would float off on the wind and the heavier grain kernels would fall back onto the blanket. As Keats watches the winnowing, the chaff comes to seem for him the bright golden hair of an earth goddess. Not all students can be expected to know how cider is made, and so the teacher or, better, another student will need to explain Keats's allusion to the cider-press. The assignment period will also give the teacher a chance to demonstrate unobtrusively an advantage of dictionary study. The etymology of *conspire* allows Keats, who was a competent Latin student, to suggest an added shade of meaning to the relations between the father/sun and the mother/earth and between them and their offspring.

Once the difficulties that might impede the students' response to the poem have been cleared out of the way, they can be assigned to attempt reading the poem on their own. They should be urged to visualize sharply; as a stimulus the teacher can tell them that the two lines

> While barred clouds bloom the soft-dying day,
> And touch the stubble-plains with rosy hue;

convey a clear enough picture that they should be able to draw it, and that the different drawings should look pretty much alike—for instance that they should show clouds of a particular kind which students have often seen, that the sun is in a particular place, and that even the time of day is specified. The students need not ask themselves as they read, "What does it mean?" Rather each should continually ask, "What do I see?" "What do I hear and touch?" "How do I feel?"

Presentation

To begin with, the teacher ought to resolve not to degrade the class into an oral quiz session in order to see if the students have "read the assignment." In an important sense, only a few of the students have succeeded in reading "To Autumn" yet; the teacher has good reason to hope that others will be able to read it in class after they have received help. The point is that, after undergoing the best preparatory activities which the teacher can devise for them, the students are now ready to read, to engage seriously with the poem. The teacher needs to give all possible energy to help them. It is best to begin by reading the first four lines and then asking the students what they see. If the students' responses do not adequately bring out the main images, then the teacher can read the lines again and ask what more is to be seen. Sometimes the teacher may have to wait for replies; silence, if it means that students are working through their innermost feelings about the poem and not just dawdling or dreaming, is a good thing.

At this early stage the discussion should establish these main points: (1) The lines offer a landscape which is actually seen in two perspectives; one view is very far-distant, distant enough to allow us to see the curve of the earth and to detect the sun above the horizon; the other view is a close-up which presents the wall and roof of a farm house twined about with vines. (Thatch roofs are made of deeply piled dry reeds, as thick as two feet, and thus they are natural nesting places for birds and vegetation.) (2) The sun and the earth are seen as great natural forces verging on personality; the sun is male and the earth female, and the two are lovers. By asking whether they are old lovers or new lovers, the teacher can get the students to appreciate the special quality in Keats's overall image—the blending of terrific, galactic-sized energy with tenderness, sustaining warmth, and calm. (3) The image of a family—the whole cosmic family—is completed by the vines and fruit, brought to life by the nourishing sun and earth.

Once the students have grasped the central image conveyed by the opening lines, they should be able to respond easily to the remainder of the stanza. The apples, gourds, nuts, flowers, and bees complete the family; they abundantly crown the vigor of a world-embracing affection. After the effect of this familial image sinks in, students should be ready for the question,

"What do you feel?" Their answers will probably be diverse in the particular words used, but if the reading has been successful thus far, they should all point in some way both to the feelings of exuberance and of comfort which the stanza embodies. The pedal note of the stanza is that special kind of luxuriance which combines creation with ease.

The second stanza may not require such detailed attention as the first. It is a series of easily assimilated variations on a theme of indolence. All of these images of harvesting toil not, neither do they spin. The students may notice, or it may have to be pointed out to them, that Keats omits a salient aspect of harvesting: the terribly hard work, certainly the hardest that occurs all the year on the farm. He gives us pictures of the traditional noonday nap and of the cider-maker, hypnotized to sleep by the oozing drops of apple juice. He even makes us recall that poppy seed, refined into opium, induces sleep. But he omits—deliberately suppresses perhaps—the picture of the tired thresher scratched by the grain husks cutting into his sweaty flesh, the overworked horses bleeding from fly bites, the exhausted field hand standing up once in a while, like Ruth in the Nightingale Ode, to ease a strained back. Keats chooses to emphasize the main point—the gathering-in —and he wholly ignores the minor point—the work. Only in the very last words does a sinister note intrude, the reminder that time flows over us and that we are getting old, getting ready, like the harvested fruit and grain, to die.

When students look at the images in the last stanza they should be able to understand that the arc of feeling in the poem completes itself here, and that the contentment in abundance in the first stanza, which modulates into indolence in the second, in the last stanza transforms itself into acquiescence in death. The images of death are profuse, and the students should have no trouble recognizing a number of them if the teacher follows the procedure of asking, "What is there to see?" "What is there to hear?" "How do those images make you feel?" The students can catch the movement toward death in such expressions as "soft-dying day" and "mourn" and perhaps in the image of the gathering birds. If a student suggests that the bleating lambs are now ready to be butchered, the idea should not be rejected; it is a possibility. The teacher may want to inform the class about the significance of the cricket.

The students need to attend carefully to their feelings as they read this stanza. Probably they will use the word *sad* to describe their impression. If so, the teacher can ask if the sadness is more like the feeling that they would have at the death of a respected old man who had enjoyed a full life, or of a younger person who had not had a chance to do all that he might have done. Or, more simply, the teacher can list such words as the following, and ask which are more accurately descriptive: *despair, resistance, resignation, sorrow, indifference, horror, outrage, nostalgia, disgust, weariness.* Finally, the teacher can point out that in the image of the soft-dying day, which needs complete visualization, the original impression of the family appears once again.

Unless the students have more that they want to say, explication has now gone far enough. The aim is to make the poem accessible by analyzing it, not to pulverize it. In order to make a successful reading, what the students must do now is to feel deeply and intimately, and that is an inner process which beyond a certain point is more impeded than helped by analysis.

A full reading of "To Autumn" must place the poem in the context of the student's thought- and feeling-life. The teacher can help the student to make connections between the reading of "To Autumn" and other parts of his or her experience by asking questions that elicit careful thought, questions that very possibly can lead to writing or, perhaps, to an oral presentation. Such a question is "Is 'To Autumn' a nature poem?" In a certain sense it is, but in another sense it is not, and by trying to define the term "nature poem" and to classify "To Autumn" in that respect the student may arrive at a clear macro-awareness of the poem. A question that may illuminate the genre is "What causes the difference in how we feel about 'To Autumn' and about Robert Frost's 'Stopping by Woods on a Snowy Evening'?" If the student is asked to compare Keats's images with James Whitcomb Riley's in "When the Frost Is on the Pun'kin," it may lead to the discovery of the effect of concentration and of what Keats called intensity. (Some students may honestly prefer Riley; nonetheless, they will have clarified their own ideas to themselves, which is the first step towards getting better ideas.) From the art department the teacher can probably borrow some reproductions of landscapes. If so, these can be put up about the room and students can be asked which ones best convey the feeling of Keats's ode. Keats appreciated painting, and the period in which he lived was a heyday of English landscapes in oils, watercolors, and etchings. Constable's work, which was contemporary with Keats, to my mind almost catches the spirit of "To Autumn," but it is a little more literal and photographic than Keats's poem. Earlier painters whose work Keats knew are the Frenchmen Pugin (whose landscapes seem too classically "hard" and decorated to suit the poem) and Lorrain (who is closer in spirit although a little dry). Of later painters, Monet strikes me as having Keats's attraction to sweetness, but he is somewhat too soft and evanescent to match Keats. Turner has Keats's energy and passion, and Cézanne conveys Keats's immense weight and solemnity and his feeling for objects as substantial things in themselves. Van Gogh's *Cypresses* is much too tortured, but his *Bridge at Arles* and the delicate *Souvenir de Mauve,* showing an apple tree in bloom, share with "To Autumn" a sense of the world as an embodiment of graciousness and joy. The teacher and the students can probably think of other landscapes that are apt for comparison or contrast with the ode.

Finally, the teacher should be ready to lead on their way those students who want more Keats. Good paperback selections are numerous and cheap, and some students may be willing to buy copies if the teacher recommends other poems by Keats.

7 Teaching the Short Story: Cather's "Paul's Case"

The Fineness of Cather's Art

A story used to circulate about two Southern writers, both women, who encountered each other at a cocktail party. Said one to the other, "The trouble with you, my dear, is, you can't write." There are, indeed, writers, including some renowned ones, who "can't write" in the sense of giving fluent, agreeable, and readily comprehensible expression to their ideas. Of the great American authors, Melville and Faulkner come to mind as examples, and sometimes Whitman is unnecessarily obscure and turbid. Willa Cather belongs to the opposite class. She is the kind of artist who refuses to subordinate craft to inspiration. However fine her conception is, she refuses to make the thought or the incident justify itself; always it must be fitted to an expression that not merely matches it but really embodies it. With her, as with her lifelong literary idols James, Flaubert, and Sarah Orne Jewett, the inspiration of a work is justified only when it has been fulfilled by polished and perfected execution. The following paragraph, which appears toward the end of "Paul's Case," illustrates Cather's technical virtuosity. Paul has resolved to commit suicide by throwing himself under a railroad engine, and he waits by the tracks for it to come.

> The carnations in his coat were drooping with the cold, he noticed, their red glory all over. It occurred to him that all the flowers he had seen in the glass cases that first night must have gone the same way, long before this. It was only one splendid breath they had, in spite of their brave mockery at the winter outside the glass; and it was a losing game in the end, it seemed, this revolt against the homilies by which the world is run. Paul took one of the blossoms carefully from his coat and scooped a little hole in the snow, where he covered it up. Then he dozed a while, from his weak condition, seemingly insensible to the cold.

It was not for nothing that Willa Cather taught high school English for some years. She knows all about the devices of grammar by which she can vividly imply mental conditions that cannot be explicitly stated in their full urgency, and she uses these devices with the finesse that results from total mastery. She wants to suggest the lassitude, the indifference to his own life, to which Paul has been reduced; therefore, to express his thoughts at this point she employs sentence shapes that are inherently otiose and languid. Thus, to slow down the sentences to a listless, eddying movement, she uses interrupting parenthetical expressions (". . . he noticed, . . ." ". . . it seemed, . . ."), a progressive verb form rather than a simple indicative ("were drooping" for "drooped"), expletive constructions in place of subject-verb statements ("it occurred to him that" for "he thought that," "it was only one splendid breath they had" for "they had only one splendid breath"), and loose sentences instead of periodic. (The last sentence, which like all but one in this paragraph is loose, might be made periodic and thus stronger if it read: "Then, from his weak condition, seemingly insensible to the cold, he dozed a while.") Even punctuation helps to retard the movement in this paragraph. The commas after *way* in the second sentence and after *had* in the third are not required either by the grammar or by the meaning; their sole function is to make the passage still more lethargic and despondent.

With one exception all the sentences in the paragraph contain one or more of these features. The exception is the sentence before the last: "Paul took one of the blossoms carefully from his coat and scooped a little hole in the snow, where he covered it up." In that instance, where Paul makes a small gesture of self-expression, the weakening grammatical attributes are absent, but even that sentence would be more emphatic if the word "carefully" were placed after "Paul" rather than after "blossoms," a degree of emphasis which Cather rejects, however, because it would give too heroic a quality to Paul's pathetic commiseration for the decaying flower and himself.

In contrast to the weary, faded tone of this passage describing Paul's depression is the third paragraph in the story, dealing with the appearance which Paul must make before his teachers in high school in order to get his suspension lifted.

> When questioned by the Principal as to why he was there Paul stated, politely enough, that he wanted to come back to school. This was a lie, but Paul was quite accustomed to lying; found it, indeed, indispensable for overcoming friction. His teachers were asked to state their respective charges against him, which they did with such rancor and aggrievedness as evinced that this was not a usual case. Disorder and impertinence were among the offenses named, yet each of his instructors felt that it was scarcely possible to put into words the real cause of the trouble, which lay in a sort of hysterically defiant manner of the boy's; and the contempt which they all knew he felt for them, and which he seemingly made not the least effort to conceal. . . .

And so the paragraph strides on, with crisp, rather declamatory sentences that reflect the teachers' excited indignation and Paul's cold but apprehensive self-possession. Both sides in the dispute summon all their strength, and the paragraph narrates their tense combat with vigorous, decisive speed.

Usually Cather directs this supple style of hers, so suited to expressing the nuances of consciousness, to the study of someone who imagines an ideal of life and then struggles to realize that ideal. The main interest in her fiction, the pervasive interest indeed, is in characters who discover and then try to achieve the good life in the face of adversity. In a sense this interest of hers is the ethical equivalent of her artistic preoccupation with making refractory material over into achieved form. Her heroes and heroines try to do much the same thing with their lives that Cather attempts to do with her stories about their lives—to make them perfect, not just in outline or intention but in the total fulfillment as well.

Illustrations of the characters' impulse toward imagining and then realizing the good life can by drawn from Cather's best-known fiction. The title character of *My Ántonia* is born into an impoverished immigrant family dominated by a whining mother and a meanly conniving brother, who works Ántonia like a horse. She makes her way to a little Nebraska town where she finds employment as a servant girl. There she is surrounded by temptations to waste herself in the trivialities of flirtations and flashy clothes. Later, when a seducer cheats her with a false promise of marriage, she is forced back to the bestial farm life from which she emerged. But throughout those tribulations she manages to keep alive within herself an ideal of worthy family living, and at last she fulfills that ideal in becoming a beneficent wife and mother of a loving family. The same determination to fulfill an ideal of oneself is shown in *Death Comes for the Archbishop.* Archbishop Latour preserves within himself both the gift of holiness and, what for Cather is near to holiness, the gift for civilization—even though he has to guard those gifts not only against the contaminations of delinquent priests and a savage country, but also against the cynicism which could easily arise in a cleric put in his position. But he does preserve them through a long and arduous life, and he even makes them prevail: His great cathedral in Santa Fe is the testimony to his holiness; his grove of apricots, so hard to cultivate in the new country, is the lasting symbol of his civilization which achieved more noble results in his daily life.

Cather herself sometimes becomes explicit about the determination that is required to hold fast to ideals and to make them govern one's life. Cécile, the motherless girl in *Shadows on the Rock,* looks around her as she begins to prepare dinner for her father and a guest.

> These coppers, big and little, these brooms and clouts and brushes, were tools; and with them one made, not shows or cabinet-work, but life itself. One made a climate within a climate; one made the days,—the complexion, the special flavour, the special happiness of each day as it passed; one made life.[1]

The principal object of most of her characters is to "make life," to find worthy purposes and then to achieve those purposes. Her villains, like

Ántonia's brother, never discover purposes that can elevate a life. Most of her heroes and heroines manage to find them and to make them work, but there are some who fail. In her novella *My Mortal Enemy*, the man and wife fail at last to make a good marriage, partly because the wife cannot allay anxieties about her uncle and her childhood religion which she renounced. The young man Claude in *One of Ours* fails because the luminous vision comes to him too late in his short existence. Ántonia's gentle and sensitive father fails and kills himself because he cannot endure his son's brutality and his wife's crudeness.

The hero of "Paul's Case" both succeeds and fails, or perhaps it would be truer to say that his success, such as it is, is highly ambiguous. To most readers the failure will probably be more obvious than the success. Paul dies; in fact, he never even has a plan to preserve himself, so that his flight to New York is not an escape so much as it is a simple running away. Furthermore, the ideal that motivates him is certainly much flawed. Paul is an esthete in the worst sense of the word; it is the glitter, not the revelation, of art that attracts him. What he wants from beauty is merely the alluring sensations that relieve the dullness of his life. The scene of his ushering at Carnegie Hall shows that he has no close interest in painting or in music as objects of attention; rather he likes them because they stimulate fantasies in which he can drift. It is the same with the theater. Only the rather sleazy actors and actresses interest him, not the plays. This flawed ideal of art in turn reflects a weakness —an underlying triviality—in Paul's character. He likes the shiny surfaces of things more than the substance of them. He scarcely notices the vocalist's singing, for instance, but he gloatingly studies her age, her possible romantic relationship with the conductor, her carriage, the hotel where she stays. Instead of learning to be an actor himself, he makes up stories to tell his schoolmates about his affairs with the actresses. His triviality expresses itself in ugly ways: He frequently lies, and he sneaks. Even his meager, excessively sinuous appearance suggests slyness mixed with weakness. Intellectually, physically, morally, he has no gifts at all. No one in the story likes him; probably not even the reader likes him.

But even though we do not like Paul, still we are on his side in his battles against his father and his Cordelia Street social environment, and even against his teachers. Wrong as he is, nevertheless he is much more nearly right than the people around hm, who, with bumper-sticker minds just large enough to contain the thinnest platitudes, cannot conceive why he should want to be any different from themselves. Paul's father points out for emulation a drab young man, settled down with a dull wife, who admiringly reveals that his boss still keeps regular office hours in his yacht on the Mediterranean and sends letters and instructions to his office back in Pittsburgh. That is as close as Paul's Cordelia Street neighbors can get to romance. Their nearest approach to gaiety is to joke that the red glass pitcher with blue enamel forget-me-nots, out of which Paul's sisters serve lemonade, must contain some more potent beverage. Paul cannot bear these surroundings: the gossipy neighbors with nothing really to talk about, the sanctimonious minister, his father standing at the top of the stairs late at night with his hairy legs protruding from his nightshirt (one remembers how disgusted Holden Caulfield was at the sight of his sick old teacher's thin legs). These people are not humdrum and ugly because they have to be; they actually prefer the kind of life they have made for themselves. They voluntarily choose it, take pride in it. They illustrate Aristotle's despondent remark that some men are born slaves.

And so when Paul opposes these people and hoodwinks them by stealing money and spending it (wasting it, they would say in Cordelia Street) to create briefly for himself a world of fine, bright things, our sympathies are with Paul, not with Cordelia Street. In some way we admire the courage that is implicit in his fight for happiness, and we know also that in his fight there is some wisdom, however clouded, some vision of a better kind of life than the one he has. Cordelia Street feels sorry for Paul: His father pays back the stolen money, the minister intends to reclaim "the poor motherless boy." Cordelia Street could better spare its pity for itself.

Seen in this way, "Paul's Case" is deeply ironical. On the one hand it presents a thoroughly unprepossessing character, one whom we simply dislike but who nevertheless lays a claim to our sympathy. On the other hand, it gives us a community—hard-working, earnest, decent—which we come to despise. Here Cather found a story that expresses a complex and profound reading of life, a vivid intuition of the mixture of good and bad in persons and societies. Which predominates in Paul, the good or the bad? Which in Cordelia Street? Ordinarily we imagine that we can answer such questions, but Cather's story poses them in a way that teases us out of thought. We become less confident in our judgments, but, guided by the clinically accurate yet softly elegiac prose of the final paragraphs, we learn that even the unlovely are to be loved, that, as the German mystic Novalis said, we touch heaven when we put our hands on a human.

Teaching the Story

The Teacher's Preparation

Although the amount of scholarly writing on Willa Cather hardly accords with her achievement, the quality of it is high. Much good criticism of Cather is brought together in an anthology called *Willa Cather and Her Critics,* ed. James Schroeter (Ithaca, N.Y.: Cornell University Press, 1967). In that book the essays of T. K. Whipple, E. K. Brown, Alfred Kazin, and Leon Edel should help the teacher to arrive at a solidly based appreciation of Cather's attainment. Three critics in Schroeter's collection express basically the same reservation about Cather; Granville Hicks, Lionel Trilling, and John H. Randall, III, all think that Cather had a weakness for smothering hard moral problems with fantasy. Although this view hardly applies to "Paul's Case," it may relate to such popular novels as *My Ántonia* and *Death Comes for the Archbishop,* and the teacher may want to consider it if those novels are to be introduced to the class.

All the book-length studies of Cather are interesting and valuable, but there are two very short ones which the teacher will find especially useful: David Daiches, *Willa Cather: A Critical Introduction* (Ithaca, N.Y.: Cornell University Press, 1951, and reprinted in paperback by Collier Books, 1962); and Dorothy Van Ghent, *Willa Cather,* University of Minnesota Pamphlets on American Writers, No. 7 (Minneapolis: University of Minnesota Press, 1964). Daiches's book is a magisterial work-by-work commentary, Van Ghent's an evocative archetypal study. Both are elegantly expressed.

Assignment

Although "Paul's Case" is probably too long to be read in class in its entirety, the students can be introduced to it in a way that is easier for them than an assigned out-of-class reading with no preparation. One help the teacher can give is to precede the assignment by reading portions of the story in class or by getting students to read. (They will read better and also learn more from the experience if they are given a chance to prepare their sections beforehand.) A first approach in class might be to summarize, with readings, the part of the story that comes before Paul's flight to New York, and then to ask the students what sort of continuation they think Cather will give. That question and the discussion of it may help to sustain the students' private reading.

Projects

Different students can be assigned particular paragraphs for close reading which they will present to the class. These questions will guide the reading: "Exactly what do you see and feel as you read the paragraph?" "After you have read it a number of times, does your response change in any way?" "As you become more familiar with the paragraph, do you find yourself adding any details of your own to Cather's presentation?" "If you do add such details, how do you decide that they are right or wrong?"

Students may need projects that will help them to understand Paul's disgust with his life. In assigning and supervising these projects the teacher will have to be tactful so as to keep the students' interest centered on Paul and not diverted unduly into extraneous social and political doctrines. A simple project can be arranged which should make students sensitive to differences in life-styles: Have a few students get together and compile lists of the most outstanding characteristics that would especially appeal to Paul when he visited a fashionable residential section, an elegant hotel, and an expensive department store; then the students can consider an ordinary neighborhood like Paul's and decide what details in his own environment must have aroused his repugnance. The report on this project can lead to a number of insights that reveal Paul's special deficiency and also his particular superiority to those around him. Some students may recognize Paul's weakness—his inordinate fastidiousness—and they may suggest that normal, adjusted people do not consider modest living circumstances to be inherently disagreeable. But other students may notice the redeeming feature in Paul's criticism of his neighbors, his perception that our culture is often much uglier than it needs to be. Not penury but a corrupt taste accounts for much of the ugliness that surrounds us, and certainly it is not lack of money that makes our shopping plazas garish and our public buildings brutal. The conclusion seems to be that Paul is right in his condemnations but wrong in his approvals. Although his hypersensitivity allows him to see the faults of his oafish neighbors, it blinds him to his own defects, his preference for such tinseled prettiness as the hothouse flowers under glass, his special regard for pretentious living.

Classroom Presentation

The reports on the projects can be worked into the classroom presentation whenever they are most appropriate. An activity that ought to get class discussion started along the right track is for the teacher to show some photographs of adolescent boys (these might be displayed on a bulletin board) and then to ask how well the pictures fit the students' images of Paul. The resulting discussion, which will certainly go beyond the physical, will help students to articulate their impressions of Paul's temperament and values, and as a result they will be able to compare their various constitutings and thus to augment them or otherwise modify them. Although the teacher will not want to enforce some uniform opinion about Paul, it is likely that one general view, with some private reservations, will emerge, particularly if the discussion is allowed to proceed for as long a time as the students' interest remains alive.

Once the class has gone as far as it can in specifying Paul's character, the question of evaluation will arise. Both the teacher's and the students' estimates of Paul need to be carefully and tentatively expressed, with plenty of leeway left for readers to absorb new insights and to change their minds. Probably readers will not agree at first, some considering Paul to be a contemptible cheat, others seeing him as an oppressed and helpless victim, and still others as a kind of hero. The main object at this stage is to get all the estimates clearly stated so that, as the discussion continues, the students come to see that the different views of Paul are not necessarily incompatible with each other, and that Cather has accomplished the difficult feat of delineating a complex character who, though flawed, nevertheless engages the reader's sympathy. The teacher can greatly help this understanding to emerge by giving the students information about point of view or, as it is sometimes called, narrative focus. In writing fiction, authors can select among these points of view: There is the narrative focus of the omniscient author who knows everything that takes place in the story; there is the focus of the main-character, first-person narrator; the focus of the minor-figure, first-person narrator; and the focus of authorial narration confined to the facts as known by some one character in the story. The fictional technique of point of view deeply affects the reader's understanding of a character. For instance, had Cather told this story from Paul's viewpoint, we might be more lenient in judging him than we are; if she had told the story from the father's point of view, we might be less lenient. But since she takes the omniscient author's point of view and decides to give us all the facts, but no cues as to the way we should feel about the facts, our attitude toward Paul is informed yet indecisive.

8 Teaching the Novel: Twain's *Huckleberry Finn*

Huckleberry Finn: The Kierkegaardian Dimension

The most obvious thing to say about *Huckleberry Finn* is that it is a sequel to *Tom Sawyer,* a sequel that exploits characters and situations not exhausted in the earlier novel. As with Tom's admired Dumas, Mark Twain's multi-faceted stories permit alternative treatments, and the Huck-Tom fiction develops along quite different lines in the two novels. But still, the one novel is a sequel to the other; from it derives its first impetus (the discovery of treasure) and its main characters. In the earlier novel, Twain's open and somewhat shifting point of view is appropriate to telling a humorous tale about a preadolescent, all-American boy who is quaintly mischievous without ever being deliberately bad. But it cannot expose clearly the shy fugitive who has no address and who fails to attend school, to wear decent clothes, or to observe accepted conventions of his time and place. *Huckleberry Finn* completes the story of Huck and Tom by changing the narrative focus, setting it in Huck's consciousness, and thus disclosing a deep and intricate personality that necessarily remains half-hidden amid the boyish exuberance of *Tom Sawyer.*

Tom plays a much larger role in Huck's part of the story than Huck plays in Tom's. In the earlier novel the shadowy and furtive Huck is much less firmly realized than other minor figures—simple, credulous Ben Rogers, for instance, or the rather sneaking Sid. In his own way Huck represents to the townspeople the dark forces that break out malevolently in the graveyard murder and in Injun Joe's terrible death. Respectable adults fear him and forbid their children his company, and since Huck himself keeps his distance from school and church, respectable boys like Tom and Ben see him only on the sly. In *Huckleberry Finn,* on the other hand, Tom Sawyer plays a large part. Not only does he appear prominently in the opening episodes as leader of the gang, but he dominates the last third of the novel with his bustling and romantic superintendence of Jim's escape.

Whether that conclusion seems effectual and organic will depend upon one's interpretation of the novel and one's assessment of its relation to the earlier book. We may be able to see a kind of rightness in the conclusion of *Huckleberry Finn* if we recall that the novel is a sequel, a sequel not so much to an action as to a situation—boys' relations with each other and with the larger world. In *Tom Sawyer* Twain had treated one side of boyhood—its hearty thirst for excitement, its confident search for pleasure, and its uncalculating and joyous egotism. In *Huckleberry Finn* he examines another side—the tentative reaching toward companionship, the sorting out of responsibilities, and the troubled investigation of oneself and one's surroundings. Huck can have very little place in *Tom Sawyer,* for the most distinctive features of his personality contradict the winningly cheerful atmosphere of that novel. But the situation in *Huckleberry Finn* is not quite the same. When we see Tom at close range in the concluding episode and contrast him with Huck, Huck not only grows in our estimation, but certain aspects of his character and moral achievement become clearer.

Tom Sawyer should not be dispraised in order to elevate Huck, for the difference in their characters is more a matter of kind than degree. Tom is at an egocentric stage of development, and he gives signs that, like most of us, he will never entirely outgrow it. When he, Huck, and Ben Rogers run away from St. Petersburg to Jackson's Island, Tom's motive is retaliation for Betsy Thatcher's rebuff; and when he sneaks back home at night, although he is wrung to kiss his suffering Aunt Polly in her broken sleep, still he does not leave the note that would have reassured her. After his spectacular entrance at his own funeral, he has this rebuke from Aunt Polly (Chapter XVIII): " 'Well, I don't say it wasn't a fine joke, Tom, to keep everybody suffering 'most a week so you boys had a good time, but it is a pity you could be so hard-hearted as to let *me* suffer so.' " Out of ignorance Aunt Polly is a little too severe. Tom had really intended to put the note by her bed, but at the last moment he decided not to in order to create a more sensational reappearance at his funeral. All his impulses go in the right direction, but nonetheless he ultimately subordinates another's well-being to a *coup de théâtre.*

"Il y a quelque chose dans les malheurs de nos amis que nous ne déplaît pas." For most of us that is true. Tom can enjoy his aunt's suffering in a way, and even the gentle Betsy, for a while, delights in the prospect of Tom's being flogged. But Huck gains no pleasure from the misfortunes of his friends. Just once he seems to, and that one occasion reveals much about his character. It is the time when, after being separated from Jim by the fog (Chapter XV, *Huckleberry Finn*), he tricks him into thinking that the incident had only been a dream, not a fact. After much elaboration of the supposed dream and then understanding that he has been mocked, Jim angrily and eloquently complains that his sorrow has been used to ridicule him. Huck, hurt in his turn, nurses his pride only for a few moments before seeing his fault and making a frank apology. His tenderness extends even to

the Duke and Dauphin, for he knows that they have abused him and are only "dead beats" and "rapscallions," but still he tries to warn them of their danger and feels "just sick" when he sees them tarred and feathered.

If there is any peculiarity in this difference between Tom and Huck, then it is on Huck's side, not Tom's. Huck, after all, is the outcast; and his grave concern for others' welfare and his sense of responsibility are extreme by almost any standard. The mob that tries to lynch Colonel Sherburn, as a variation on its more ordinary pleasures of setting fire to cats and tying cans to dogs' tails, represents the statistical mean of compassion in *Huckleberry Finn,* and few characters if any—perhaps not even Mary Jane Wilks—possess Huck's delicate awareness of others' chances for happiness or his conviction that he must maximize those chances.

Tom and Huck also differ in their social affinities. Aside from his boy companions, Tom feels most comfortable with Becky, Mary, Aunt Polly, and Aunt Sally—conventional middle-class females who, without much character of their own, enthusiastically admire boyish ebullience. But Huck, who usually responds blankly to such people,[1] naturally and easily associates with those who sink below the social average, and also, rather surprisingly in the light of his own origins, those who rise high above it. It is not easy to imagine the obstreperous and light-minded Tom fitting as contentedly into the Grangerford household as Huck does. Huck is not ironical when he says after the lynch mob ran away from Colonel Sherburn, he himself could have stayed had he wanted to. In fact, he could have stayed, for he and Sherburn have something in common that distinguishes them from the others: They are the only ones who stand apart from the mob and feel their own identity as separate persons. They are, in their different ways, both aristocrats.

They are not aristocrats of the same kind, of course. Sherburn, to use Huck's terms, is "quality," "has blood," and Huck conspicuously lacks these attributes. Nonetheless, the special nobility of Huck's character assimilates him more closely to the Sherburns and Grangerfords than to such middle-class people as the Wilkses and the Phelpses. Sherburn is placed above the mob by virtue of moral and intellectual refinement; Huck's nobility stems from his determined pursuit of a goal that carries him far beyond ordinary social affiliations and eventually outside the physical boundaries of the novel altogether. Huck's final move to the Indian Territory, like Abraham's pilgrimage to Mount Moriah in Sören Kierkegaard's account, expresses a unique spiritual adjustment which replaces the norms of social intercourse with a transcendent and terrifyingly immediate acquaintance with supernatural force. Kierkegaard took Abraham as the type of the "knight of faith," and the outlines of Huck's experience are close enough to Abraham's to suggest that he too belongs to this order of aristocracy, not of blood but of spirit.[2]

Movement Toward Faith

Kierkegaard distinguishes his spiritual knights from ordinary men by their
being lifted above a mediated relation to the universal (which is the realm of
ethics), to a particular and immediate relation to the absolute (which is the
realm of metaphysics and religion). This conception, which is crucial to his
thought, he expresses several times, but the following passage is perhaps
the clearest statement (p. 80):

> The paradox of faith is this, that the individual is higher than the
> universal, that the individual (to recall a dogmatic distinction now rather
> seldom heard) determines his relation to the universal by his relation
> to the absolute, not his relation to the absolute by his relation to the
> universal. The paradox can also be expressed by saying that there is an
> absolute duty toward God; for in this relationship of duty the individual
> as an individual stands related absolutely to the absolute.

The demands which the absolute makes upon the rare person who is fit
to sustain its imperatives may not be the same as the ethical norms of
universal social experience, and so it is, in the case of Abraham, that (p. 41)
"the ethical expression of what Abraham did is, that he would murder Isaac:
the religious expression is, that he would sacrifice Isaac . . . ." One who must
endure such a conflict between received values and directly intuited com-
mands undergoes a terrific spiritual transformation which Kierkegaard calls
dread, and so Kierkegaard concludes this sentence about Abraham's willingness to kill Isaac by remarking, "But precisely in this contradiction consists
the dread which can well make a man sleepless, and yet Abraham is not
what he is without this dread."

The first step which the knight of faith takes toward his ultimate
spiritual condition is a resignation amounting to positive acceptance. Resignation is an act in which the knight, in one intense moment, accedes to
some terrible requirement and thus concentrates for himself the whole
spiritual significance of his life. Kierkegaard emphasizes the holistic character
of this experience, the epitomizing, in one capital and symbolic moment, of
all that the knight is spiritually. Thus he remarks (pp. 53–54):

> So, for the first thing, the knight will have power to concentrate
> the whole content of life and the whole significance of reality in one
> single wish. If a man lacks this concentration, if his soul from the
> beginning is dispersed in the multifarious, he never comes to the point of
> making the movement, he will deal shrewdly in life like the capitalists
> who invest their money in all sorts of securities, so as to gain on the
> one what they lose on the other—in short, he is not a knight. In the next
> place the knight will have the power to concentrate the whole result of
> the operations of thought in one act of consciousness. If he lacks this
> intensity, if his soul from the beginning is dispersed in the multifarious,

he will not get time to make the movements, he will be constantly
running errands in life, never enter into eternity, for even at the instant
when he is closest to it he will suddenly remember that he has forgotten
something for which he must go back.

Once made, this act of resignation indelibly marks the soul, and out of the
dread in this terrible moment evolves a calm (p. 56): "In the infinite resignation there is peace and rest . . . ." But even though total resignation to the
absolute's decree, with its separation from the comforts of conventional
wisdom and experience, is a remarkable and distinctive act, still it is
supplemented in cases of highest spiritual development by one further
movement of the soul. When discussing this further movement, faith proper,
Kierkegaard almost always invokes the absurd. The final movement of faith
is a settled conviction, not just a velleity or a fantasy that, in fact, all will be
well, that the violation of received and intelligible norms has an ultimate and
infinite rightness. In the case of Abraham, about to plunge the knife into
Isaac, his faith was the absurd certainty, even accompanying the terrible
pain of his act, that he would not really lose his son (p. 46): "All that
time [of the journey] he believed—he believed that God would not require
Isaac of him, whereas he was willing nevertheless to sacrifice him if it was
required. He believed by virtue of the absurd; for there could be no question
of human calculation, and it was indeed the absurd that God who required
it of him should the next instant recall the requirement."

Kierkegaard's outline of the knight of faith's progress shows three main
phases: (1) The knight confronts the whole spiritual significance of his life in
one dreadful moment. In that moment the absolute requires from him some
shockingly painful capitulation to a demand which affronts the moral
decencies that he previously had trusted. (Abraham must kill Isaac.)
(2) Although agonized by his situation, the knight acknowledges the superior
truth of this call, freely assents to the requirement, and thereby finds peace.
(Abraham resigns himself to the command.) (3) Beyond this acceptance of
the dreadful sacrifice, one more act remains. It is the conviction, in spite of
all apparent contradiction, that the right order of things is preserved. (Even
as he goes about the sacrifice, Abraham believes that he will not lose Isaac.)

Huck's Spiritual Development

When Twain wrote *Huckleberry Finn*, his mind seems to have moved in a
direction parallel to Kierkegaard's, for Huck's spiritual development recapitu-
lates the main stages of Abraham's. The equivalent for Huck of Abraham's
test over Isaac occurs in Chapter XXI; it is the crisis of deciding whether to
send Miss Watson the letter that would return Jim to slavery. After writing
his letter, Huck recalls the trip down the river and remembers the touching

proofs of Jim's affection. At that instant he glances at the letter, and he recognizes the overriding symbolic significance to him of the decision that he must now make.

> It was a close place. I took it up and held it in my hand. I was a trembling, because I'd got to decide, forever, betwixt two things, and I knowed it. I studied it for a minute, sort of holding my breath. . . .

Then, like Abraham, he renounces conventional morality (returning Jim to his owner) and deliberately resigns himself to the command that appears to him and all its spiritual consequences.

> . . . and then I says to myself:
> "All right, then, I'll *go* to hell"—and tore it up. It was awful thoughts, and awful words, but they was said.

Then Huck takes the final step which makes him a knight of faith: He affirms the rightness of the spiritual state to which his decision about Jim has brought him. In the next sentences, restricted to the language that he knows, Huck speaks of himself as a perpetual delinquent. But these sentences really stress meekness, not rebellion; they proclaim Huck's firm attachment to a mode of living which he recognizes to be the right one for him, however much the common view may contradict it. Having successfully passed his crisis, he affirms his spiritual sanity and independence, his special relation to the absolute:

> And let them stay said: and never thought no more about reforming. I shoved the whole thing out of my head; and said I would take up wickedness again, which was in my line, being brung up to it, and the other warn't.

Certain aspects of the novel take on special significance when they are seen from the standpoint of Huck's spiritual attainment. The last episode contrasts Huck and Tom and the life-styles which they illustrate. Tom's soul, joyous and egocentric, is dispersed in the multifarious excitements of his escapade; Huck, concentrated on a single dedication, moves in a straight line toward his own and Jim's freedom. Deeply cemented into the social structure, Tom accepts without question the morals of his time and place. From the beginning he knows about Miss Watson's will, but he pretends to set Jim free, innocently yet brutally careless of the immorality of his practical joke. Although Huck lies as much as Tom, he is incapable of such gross deceit. Having faith, in the Kierkegaardian sense, that freeing Jim is ultimately right, regardless of conventional moral views, he acts wholeheartedly. In fact, Huck's faith is justified in much the same way as Abraham's, for just as God at the last moment remits the command to Abraham, so finally it appears that Jim's freedom has acquired social (legal) status through Miss Watson's will.

Twain does not use this implied contrast to disparage Tom, who is a "good boy" in the conventional and agreeable sense. Rather, the contrast works to show that Huck, who certainly is not a "good boy," is altogether a different and uncommon breed of man. When Twain wrote *Huckleberry Finn* his sympathies were still wide, but already he gave hints of the direction his heart would go as, in the later years, it darkened and hardened.

A note of the knight of faith is inwardness, and a characteristic which Huck shares with the other bona fide aristocrats of the novel—Sherburn, the Grangerfords, and the Shepherdsons—is the ability to set himself apart from his environment, even to see himself as opposed to it. Huck and the social aristocrats are not naive egoists like Tom, but they have a more acute sense of their own identity than the other characters have. The Duke and the Dauphin, false aristocrats, closely link themselves to the world by making it their prey; the Wilkses, Phelpses, and Tom and his family weave intricate bonds of affection and good works between themselves and others; the Arkansas hillbillies never surmount a swinish congeniality with their immediate surroundings. But Huck and the other aristocrats refuse to sink into unreflecting dependence upon circumstances.

Huck merely resembles the social aristocrats, however; essentially he differs from them almost as much as he does from Tom. His inwardness, which is spiritual rather than social, goes far beyond the other aristocrats' aloofness. This inwardness, like Abraham's, is a special relation to the absolute, and since that relation is incommensurable with anyone else's experience, it sets the knight of faith apart from his neighbors. Kierkegaard discusses this separation in a lengthy chapter ("Problem III: Was Abraham ethically defensible in keeping silent before Sarah, before Eleazar, before Isaac?"), and his point is that Abraham cannot cross the spiritual gap between himself and others simply because the ordinary person cannot possibly understand his climactic experiences.

So the knight of faith retires from social intercourse in order to take up another communion, and Huck's last sentences are: "But I reckon I got to light out to the Territory before the rest,[3] because Aunt Sally she's going to adopt me and sivilize me and I can't stand it. I been there before." Huck's voluntary withdrawal is not alienation; rather it is obedience. Huck has no grudge against civilization, but having "been there before," he knows that it interferes with his own special call. He leaves social, even personal, relations therefore by choice and not from any sense of loneliness or rejection. Huck's reward for having passed a great spiritual crisis is that he can now confidently take what he has learned to want.

Knights of faith are God's slaves but not men's. Since their unquestioning fidelity in the one world totally liberates them in the other, they are prime mythic and epic material. They address the imagination by perfectly representing certain maximum ideals of behavior because, being wholly free really to achieve those ideals, they actually embody them. Loner though he is, Huck comes to incarnate, before the novel is finished, an ideal of civility which Lionel Trilling calls *community*[4] but which, without stretching terms, may also be called love. That Huck has learned to love becomes apparent when his attitude toward adults at the beginning of the novel is compared to his feelings about them later. At the outset he is cheekily contemptuous of the Widow Douglas and Old Miss Watson, and his descriptions of their manners and beliefs is frankly mocking. He softens nothing in the portrait he draws of his degenerate Pap, and he does not even trust Judge Thatcher enough to explain to him plainly that he wants him to obtain legal possession of Huck's share of the treasure money in order to safeguard it from Pap. He cheerfully cooperates with Tom to victimize Jim with low tricks that rob him of adult dignity and bring him down to the boys' own level.

But by the middle of the novel a change in this distrustful attitude toward adults has come about. To be sure, Huck never becomes sentimental, and he still finds many around him to despise and suspect; mainly he lies, for instance, in order to protect himself from such human predators as the robbers in the *Walter Scott* and the men who hunt the river for escaped slaves to capture and return for reward money. So, although Huck's standards of decent conduct prevent him from accepting the shiftless loungers in an Arkansas river town or the lynch mob, still he can see through the bungling ineptitude of Uncle Silas to the essential sweetness and strength that lie beneath (Chapter XXXVII): "He was a mighty nice old man. And always is." A more striking sign of Huck's changed attitude is his outright admiration for Colonel Grangerford and his handsome sons, and for the courageous Colonel Sherburn, who stands off an entire mob. They become heroes to him, models for gallantry and spirit. He manages to adapt those aristocratic virtues to his own humble circumstances when he counteracts the machinations of the Duke and Dauphin so as to protect Mary Jane Wilks, another adult whom he honors.

The experience that taught Huck the capacity to respect deserving adults rather than automatically despising them all is the life with Jim on the river. As they float along, "borrowing" fruit and vegetables and an occasional chicken, fending off slave stealers and other crooks, delighting in the idyllic contentment of free conversation varied with a smoke and a swim, Huck gradually and insensibly becomes closely attached to Jim. That attachment goes much farther with Huck than any relationship that he has entered before. It goes so far, in fact, as to become a dependency relationship, a condition in which Huck's happiness depends upon Jim's approving him and his actions. Huck first discovers how much has has come to need Jim's approval in the previously mentioned episode in Chapter XV, when Jim rebukes Huck for making a fool of him. Often before in the novel, Huck has been reprimanded by an adult, but previously he has always withstood adult criticism—Pap's, Old Miss Watson's, and others'—with smirking mockery. With Jim, however, he acknowledges, for the first time, that his happiness depends upon another being. "It was fifteen minutes before I could work myself up to go and humble myself to a nigger—but I done it, and I warn't ever sorry for it afterwards, neither." After that first occasion when he accepts rather than resists a serious call to love and the duties that love entails, Huck's self-identification and self-definition advance rapidly, for he can respond to others along an entirely new dimension. His past experience protects him from being duped by the charlatans he meets, and his newly acquired desire to get the approval of those he likes opens up to him models for his own development. So he is able to absorb into his own emerging character the aristocrats' self-sufficiency, Jim's delicacy of feeling, Uncle Silas's long-suffering, Aunt Polly's responsibility.

Huckleberry Finn is both serious and cheerful. It is a novel about growing up which describes an unusually successful case of soul-making. Although it sees its subject in much the same way as *Fear and Trembling,* it complements that work by featuring the joyousness, contentment, and growth which Kierkegaard acknowledged as the knight's final lot, but which he mainly ignored in attending to the spiritually appalling process by which the knight attains his ultimate communion.

Teaching the Novel

A Special Problem

Huckleberry Finn has always been, for one reason or another, a dangerous book to teach. It is dangerous enough that some teachers stay away from it altogether except to put it on their lists of recommended or supplementary readings. But *Huckleberry Finn* is not in the same category with the licentious Miller's Tale, which Chaucer recommended the reader to set aside, if it offended him, and choose another. For in American literature there is no other tale to choose that has the status of this novel, and perhaps no other tale whatever that expresses so powerfully and wisely some of the most basic issues concerning freedom, human dignity, and personal responsibility. In addition, it is one of the most teachable of the great works; one does not so much teach it as merely give it to students.

Nonetheless, in the present social condition, the book offers a special teaching problem that will be difficult in nearly all situations, but which will be insuperable in others, in which the teacher will have to forego this great novel, however regretfully. The problem is Twain's depiction of an attitude of condescension, which he himself did not share, toward the black—an attitude in which the black himself was caught up. The problem is illustrated at a simple level by use of the word *nigger,* which appears fairly often. If that were all, then the difficulty could be overcome easily enough by the teacher's pointing out the fact that, historically, words go up and down in respectability and that in the period covered in *Huckleberry Finn, nigger* did not necessarily express opprobrious connotations among the people who used it: Jim himself says the word in referring to blacks. Unfortunately, however, there is more to it than that. The chief characters in the novel really do consider blacks to be an inferior race, and the evidence goes beyond the occasional use of a now offensive term. The kind and generous Aunt Sally asks Huck if anyone was hurt in a steamboat accident (Chapter XXII), and when Huck replies " 'No'm. Killed a nigger.' "she says, " 'Well, it's lucky; because sometimes people do get hurt.' " In a moment of exasperation with Jim, Huck himself says, "You can't learn a nigger to argue." (Chapter XIV), and when he sees Jim suffering because of his separation from his wife and children, he wonderingly remarks (Chapter XXIII), "and I do believe he cared just as much for his people as white folks does for ther'n. It don't seem natural, but I reckon it's so." Even Jim seems to respect his own race less than he does whites. If a man spoke French to him, Jim would " 'take en bust him over de head. Dat is, if he warn't white.' " (Chapter XIV).

This racist bias which runs all through the novel is one aspect of Twain's pervasive irony. Thus Aunt Sally, a thoroughly decent woman who treats her black slaves with the same rough but kindly indulgence which she accords everyone in her family, is nonetheless incapable of the theoretical notion that the races are humanly equal, and Huck himself can only account for Jim's merit by supposing that he is greatly superior to the average of blacks (as indeed he is, and to whites too—though that reflection does not occur to Huck). The irony in Twain's description of racial relations reaches its height of sinister complexity in the last chapters of the novel, the ones that recount the effort to free Jim. Huck, understanding only the surface of the episode, supposes that the "good" Tom Sawyer is actually bent on the crime of freeing (or stealing) Jim, an act so vicious in Huck's mind that even he attempts it fearfully. But what Huck does not know—and Tom does—is that Jim is already free, having been set free by Miss Watson's will, and thus that Tom is doing no wrong except to practice upon others' credulity so as to enslave a free man. Then, when all the facts come out, Huck is relieved—relieved because he understands at last that Tom was not a bad boy like himself, a "nigger stealer," after all! Irony indeed.

If Aunt Sally and Tom and the rest were merely nineteenth century versions of Archie Bunker, no teaching problem would arise, for our students would understand easily enough the simple paradox of mildly venal people who do not see their surroundings accurately because of prejudice. But Twain's characters are not Archie Bunkers, and his novel does not deal in harmless banalities. In its treatment of the race question, *Huckleberry Finn* will almost certainly offend some students; some particular action or statement of opinion, even though Twain himself despises it, will so outrage them that they will be unable to judge it dispassionately in its context and see it for what it is, but instead will condemn the whole novel and its author for bigotry. A treatment of racial tension which takes account of many different facts and social environments and many points view is almost certain to give offense to some, just because it is many-sided, for strongly committed people do not always welcome a complex and ironical discussion of a moral issue even when that discussion supports their own principles.

If a teacher knows that the students are tense about the issue of race, then it is better not to try to teach them *Huckleberry Finn*. It is a question of readiness; students who cannot take a serious stand on a moral question and at the same time realize that this stand can be supported in more ways than one are not intellectually ready for this novel. Teachers should not judge students harshly, for combining commitment with tolerance is never easy.

In many cases, for instance in large city high schools where there is a mixed ethnic population and where racial relations are strained, the teacher should probably not even consider this novel for classroom use. On the other hand, *Huckleberry Finn* is so great in itself and, barring the possible misunderstanding of Twain's attitude toward race, so well suited to students' capacities and needs, that a high school teacher will at least want to try to introduce it if there is a good chance for success. The attempt can best be made by straightforwardly describing the problem to the students and honestly leaving them to decide whether or not to read the book. The teacher should mention Twain's use of the word *nigger* and explain that Twain's characters, not Twain himself, use it. It should be explained that even the normally civil characters in *Huckleberry Finn* were unable to conceive of blacks as equals with whites, and that Huck's own eventual transcendence of this attitude is incomplete and expressed in words that offend a modern reader of liberal views. The teacher should also explain why it is desirable to read the novel with them in spite of these disagreeable features. Finally, a few students can be asked to read the novel beforehand, or parts of it, for the rest of the class and give advice. Then the class should be ready to decide. If teachers use this same procedure with other potentially controversial works, they will be able to avoid selections that are unteachable in class because of a content that students cannot yet handle.

If the teacher can successfully get through the painful duty of preparing students for encountering the racial aspect of *Huckleberry Finn,* then everything else will be pure delight. There are many points of entry into this novel, and they all work. The following paragraphs suggest some approaches, but every teacher who likes this novel will think of different ones, and still other ideas will quite possibly spring up in class, spontaneously offered by students.

The Teacher's Preparation

The quantity of writing on Mark Twain is so great that the nonspecialist can only sample it. A collection of essays by various writers is Guy A. Cardwell, ed., *Discussions of Mark Twain* (Boston: D. C. Heath and Company, 1963); another is Henry Nash Smith, ed., *Mark Twain: A Collection of Critical Essays* (Englewood Cliffs, N.J.: Prentice-Hall, 1963). Both books bring together very good writing, and between the two books only one article is repeated. There are two casebooks on *Huckleberry Finn:* Richard Lettis, Robert F. McDonnell, and William Morris, eds., *Huck Finn and His Critics* (New York: Macmillan Company, 1962) and Hamlin Hill and Walter Blair, eds., *The Art of Huckleberry Finn: Text, Sources, Criticisms* (San Francisco: Chandler Publishing Company, 1962). These two publications give the text of the novel, a sampling of criticism of it, and lists of questions to focus reflection and writing. They are useful to the teacher because they provide good criticism and also because they offer ideas for approaching the novel in class. An article not included in any of these collections but well worth looking up is Cleanth Brooks, "The Teaching of the Novel: *Huckleberry Finn*" in *Essays on the Teaching of English: Reports of the Yale Conferences on the Teaching of English,* eds., Edward J. Gordon and Edward S. Noyes (New York: Appleton-Century-Crofts, 1960), pp. 203–215.

Audiovisual Aids

Out of the ample field of audiovisual material on *Huckleberry Finn,* the teacher should certainly not miss Hal Holbrook's splendid recording called *Mark Twain Tonight* (Columbia Records, OL5440). This record is fine entertainment, but it is also vital, deeply sympathetic criticism. Take, for instance, the section in which Holbrook imitates Mark Twain, on the lecture circuit, reading from his own *Huckleberry Finn.* The delicate, subtle shifts and dodges in the narrative point of view are made palpable for all as, in the prime of his own creative life, Holbrook imitates the aged Twain's representation of the thirteen-year-old Huck as he mimics his depraved Pap. The truths of *Huckleberry Finn* come to us strained and purified through layer upon layer of prejudice, experience, judgment, reservation, and revision, and we ourselves never know just where we stand as we watch Huck picking his way through the labyrinth toward self-discovery. All this complication in the discovery of truth, and in the truths themselves which are the object of the search, Holbrook is able to make plain, not by analysis but by immediate presentation.

The teacher will probably want to select some visual aids which show the Mississippi River Valley in Huck's time—and in our own time, since the immemorial as well as the fleeting quality of the river enters into Twain's theme. Students can certainly be recruited to do some of the work of selection and presentation. In their social science studies and in their casual reading they can be on the look-out for appropriate illustrations, and in addition some of the projects and activities which appear below should lead them into relevant material of different kinds. In his painting *Huck Finn and Nigger Jim,* Thomas Hart Benton finely evokes the warmth of thorough trust, and if the teacher can get a copy of it, the picture will make a central item for a bulletin board. Incidentally, a student who reads *Huckleberry Finn* closely may be able to catch two small errors in detail which Benton makes: Jim should have a "hairy breas'," and the steamboat in the background, which must be going upstream since a raft floats past it in the opposite direction, should be hugging the river bank rather than pushing up the middle.

Oral Work

Oral work, for classes that are adept at it, is another entrance into *Huckleberry Finn.* Many chapters are ideal for reading aloud both by the teacher and by the students, if they are ready for it and have been given such help as listening first to the teacher's or Holbrook's reading and have been told in advance that they will read. Impersonating Huck requires thoughtful consideration of his character, for his speech combines cynicism with the special innocence of a boy who is both ignorant and intelligent, timid but on occasion brave, distrustful but generous. A number of the episodes can lead to role-playing and dramatization if the teacher and the class are equal to those procedures. Huck's trying to imitate a girl (Chapter XI), Huck's spying on the robbers in the *Walter Scott* (Chapter XII), the Dauphin's "working" a camp meeting (Chapter XX), the rehearsal by the Duke and Dauphin of a performance (Chapter XXI), and Sherburn's repulsing of the mob and Huck's visit to the circus (Chapter XXII) are only a few of the many incidents that allow dramatic treatment. Girls will find opportunities for role-playing in Colonel Grangerford's spirited daughters (Chapters XVII and XVIII) and in ludicrous Sister Hotchkiss (Chapter XLI).

Projects

Projects which should illuminate this work are not hard to find. Two or three students can discover what more is known about Hucklebery Finn than the novel itself tells. One resource for this project, of course, is *Tom Sawyer,* a more simply constructed book which students can master without the teacher's help. Another resource is the long chapter describing Huck's adventure on a lumber raft, which Twain rejected from *Huckleberry Finn* but included in *Life on the Mississippi*. In addition, something is known about the real-life model for Huck. Another project, for students with interests in history or debate, can deal with the various attempts at suppression which the novel has undergone. Here are some relevant questions: "Why has *Huckleberry Finn* been a 'banned book' from time to time?" "What ideas in the novel conflict with commonly held views about morality, race relations, the worth of the common man?" "When does Twain use a character to expound his own ideas; when does Twain himself disagree with his characters' thoughts?" "How can you tell that Twain agrees with a character or disagrees with him?" ("Is Twain as contemptuous of the 'common man,' for instance, as Colonel Sherburn is?")

Other projects can help students to see characters sharply and to feel the episodes intimately. One such project involves attempts to visualize the characters, and it can absorb the energies of four or five students who are endowed with different talents. The teacher can select a student group that includes at least one observant reader, one or two students who like to draw, and one who, interested in fashion or in history, is willing to read books on nineteenth century customs and dress. The project asks the students to discover the appearance of such figures as Huck's Pap, Judge Thatcher, and Colonel Grangerford and his daughters. The novel itself can be read carefully for descriptions, and the information which Twain expected his contemporaries to know can be found in works of social history; then this information can be brought together in drawings of some of the leading characters, and the class as a whole can examine these drawings and make suggestions and criticisms. Much the same sort of project can be applied to appreciating Huck's awed comment about one of the grander Mississippi steamboats: "She had a power of style to her." That project can explain why a Mississippi steamboat was such an impressive sight, not only to Huck but to much more worldly characters as well. Students working on this project can find valuable information in Twain's masterly *Life on the Mississippi*. Still another project in visualization can portray the kind of life which Huck and Jim enjoyed once they had finally put their raft in good condition. By itself *Huckleberry Finn* provides ample written material for this project, but students can supplement it imaginatively. A diagram of the raft, together with such a log book as Huck might write (notes for his eventual account that Mr. Twain edited), would make a good bulletin board display for instance— one that could suggest short stories and vignettes about Huck's and Jim's life on the river.

Naturally the teacher will want to arrange these projects in a way that contributes as fully as possible to the students' successful reading of the novel. Much depends on the maturity of the class—its reading level, its variety of interests, its ability to investigate independently—and much also depends on the teacher's particular style, experience, and familiarity with Twain. One teacher may want to set aside a period of time when the projects can be offered sequentially; another may prefer that they be brought in separately and incidentally, in connection with class discussions that can rely on them for information and ideas. In some situations formal presentations may work best; in others, students who have worked on a particular project can best contribute their findings informally as part of regular class discussion.

In any case, students will need time to study their project assignments, and they also will need the teacher's guidance. Some of the time can come from traditional homework, but in addition students will need regular class time in order to agree with each other about their respective duties and to consult library references. This class time spent on projects will give the teacher a chance to guide the students, to inform them about library resources that go beyond the *Encyclopedia Britannica* and the *Readers' Guide,* and to see to it that students are really keeping to the main line of profitable investigation rather than being lured into detours and morasses.

Reading the Novel as a Whole Work

Although a novel is long and divides itself into parts, nonetheless it is one work and demands one total response, or set of responses, from the reader. But on the other hand, all the pedagogical exigencies are for cutting it up into bits and pieces, in assignments of twenty-odd pages a day—a program that can stretch the reading period to three weeks. So a gap arises between what the novel demands as a work of art, and what students, with only a period a day for English and many other requirements besides, are able to give to it. Somehow or other the teacher must arrange experiences that fill that gap. Projects will help to a certain extent since they direct attention to aspects of the work that transcend a day's reading assignment. The teacher's questions are another means of helping students to respond to the whole work. If the questions knit reading installments together by pertaining to continuous elements of plot and theme, then they will help the student to pull the reading into one piece. Some of the following questions should do that. They can be discussed day after day as the students acquire information in their reading, and thus they can help to unify the students' experience of the work.

1. How old is Huck? (Twain finally gives an approximate answer— "thirteen or fourteen or along there"—in Chapter XVII. Students may have guessed Huck to be younger than that.)

2. What are Huck's feelings about Jim in each reading section? What has happened to his feelings about Jim in the course of their journey?

3. Draw a long vertical line and then put on this line the principal characters who appear in each reading section, placing them high or low or toward the middle according to Huck's estimate of their worth. Then see if the chart helps you to answer these questions. Does Huck hate anyone to the extent that he wishes that person harm? Is Huck generally distrustful of people? Do Huck's views of people become harsher or softer as the novel progresses? Are there any characters whom Huck admires in some way but at the same time despises? Are there any whom he dislikes but wants to protect?

4. In this novel who are the people who look down on Huck, which ones look up to him, and which ones ignore him?

5. Imagine Huck and Tom twenty years later than the time recounted in the novel. Can you imagine either one or the other of them or both fitting into any of the following roles?

congressman	soldier	diplomat
lawyer	writer	policeman
hermit	farmer	gangster
minister	card-shark	philosopher
family man	businessman	pioneer
drunkard	teacher	inventor

6. What lies, and how many, does Huck tell? Why does he tell lies? Does he ever tell lies that hurt anyone? Do any other characters ever succeed in deceiving him?

This question at the end of the reading may help students to review some ethical implications in the novel: "Was Huck right to decide to 'light out,' or should he have decided to stay with Aunt Sally?"

9 Teaching the Drama: Shakespeare's *Othello*

Iago's Guilt and Othello's

If we are to read the play that Shakespeare wrote we must acknowledge that Othello as well as Iago commits great evil. The phrase that Coleridge employed to explain Iago's behavior—"motiveless malignity"—has a deep truth, both as applied to Iago's destructiveness and also to Othello's. The malignity that never tires of hurting and degrading is necessarily without motive in that it exceeds whatever motive eventually lies behind it.

The special terror that a good presentation of *Othello* ought to produce in its audience arises from the fact that the savagery of the two central characters cannot in any way be satisfactorily explained—even though their wildness is thoroughly probable, consistent with the loss of conscience that appears in some persons when they are placed in the conditions of life that surround Othello and Iago. Most people can reasonably well control their behavior most of the time with the assistance of social conventions, a degree of personal security, and various releases of emotional stress. But Othello and Iago depict the unhappy state of human beings who have been bereft of those supports, which exist for these two characters much less fully than for others in the play. Social conventions do not serve to hold them in check because, in Othello's case, he is not only a foreigner, like Cassio, but he is also a product of a radically different culture from the one in which he lives—and as for Iago, his opportunistic cynicism alienates him from all others, whom he contemptuously regards as his gulls. These two men also lack a normal degree of security. Othello, in spite of his high rank, is only a mercenary after all, and Iago smarts under the insult of having been denied what he considers to be his due position. Both characters, moreover, lack those emotional contacts with others which help to soften aggressive behavior, for they are both of them immensely private men who do not freely communicate their deepest feelings. Iago is even proud that he does not "wear my heart upon my sleeve / For daws to peck at," (I, i, 64–65), whereas Othello's attempt at intimate communion—his marriage—nearly succeeds but in fact ends in disaster, precisely because at the crucial moment he cannot put his whole trust in another.

Consequently, the terrible acts which Iago and Othello commit ought to arouse in a sensitive audience a considerably different response from that which the crimes of characters in Shakespeare's other great tragedies evoke. Comparison with Macbeth illustrates the difference. Macbeth's crimes—the murdering of children for instance—are horrible, but nonetheless they have an objective sense in them once Macbeth's object of seizing and maintaining power is granted. Thus we can make a moral judgment upon Macbeth, and we can express it in a form that reflects our consciously held ethical principles. We can say, for instance, that Macbeth overvalues the good of holding power but undervalues the good of other people's well-being. But with Othello and Iago this factual and logical basis for judgment of the characters is missing, for their malignity, being motiveless, loses touch with the original intention behind it. Macbeth, for example, knows very well why he kills Lady Macduff and her son: he does it to secure his power. But Iago and Othello, by contrast, have lost the sanity to balance one good against another and then decide on a rational and deliberate course of action, right or wrong morally. Wandering uncertainly in a phantasmagoria made of their own powerful but deluded feelings, they so misunderstand the real world that they stumble blindly past the facts. So, when they give their reasons for behaving as they do, they talk nonsense: Iago believes that Othello had an affair with Emilia; Othello is convinced that Desdemona has committed adultery with Cassio even though all the events since the landing on Cypress are compressed into a period of time—the afternoon and night of one day and the morning, afternoon, and evening of the next—that would have made their sleeping together impossible.

The mistakes that Othello's unstable feelings cause him to make are obvious as well as terrible, but Iago also makes mistakes. It was simply foolish of him, for instance, just after the seeming death of Roderigo, to send Emilia off to inform Othello, for had she arrived a moment sooner the murder of Desdemona could not have occurred. Iago cannot see things as they exist and deal with them realistically because his feelings, especially his inflamed hostility, obscure the world for him. Othello, too, after his emotional and moral breakdown in the third act, comes to suffer the same blindness and the same incapacity. So when we ask, as we always ask about characters in a drama, why they act as they do, we must expect the answers to refer more to these characters' contorted perceptions than to the world in which Shakespeare makes them live.

Explaining Iago's Actions

Iago provides two reasons to explain his hatred of Othello and Cassio. One is that Othello has promoted Cassio over himself, who had the greater length of service, so that Iago is merely Cassio's subordinate. This reason for hostility must be taken seriously. Iago's account of the matter, which occurs in the opening speeches of the play, splutters with rage and a sense of injured merit. Anyone who has been in the army or any other hierarchical institution will recognize the arguments and also the rancor in Iago's diatribe: Cassio's knowledge of warfare, Iago claims, is all theoretical and learned from books; Iago's is real and based on experience. Cassio has seen less service than Iago. Cassio has not, like Iago, served in combat directly under Othello's command. Iago's complaint goes straight to the bitter observation that has been repeated down through the ages by disappointed officers, teachers, bureaucrats, clergymen:

> Why there's no remedy; 'tis the curse of the service,
> Preferment goes by letter and affection,
> Not by the old gradation, where each second
> Stood heir to the first.[1]

(I, i, 35–38)

The outrage seems genuine enough, and the grounds for it are plausible; we still hear these arguments and give them some weight. What must especially gall Iago in Cassio's success is that it results not from just Othello's approval but from others' as well. Thus, at the end of the play, Cassio is advanced still higher to be governor of Cyprus, by official action of the Venetian Senate. Othello and Cassio live in a realm of responsibility and therefore of dignity where Iago will never be admitted. They are big men, he a small man. His knowledge that "We cannot all be masters" (I, i, 43) leads him defiantly to insist that as long as he must be a servant, he will not be a faithful one "doting on his own obsequious bondage" (46) but rather will look out for himself while only seeming to serve his masters.

Up to a point there is nothing unusual in Iago's feelings or his expression of them. The fact that "We cannot all be masters" is hard for most of us to accept, especially when we find ourselves in immediate contact with one of those masters. And, beyond that, most of us are inclined to mock our superiors sometimes, and perhaps even to pull them down a peg or two if we can. Moreover, we feel that the impulse is wholesome, since no human should be placed unreachably above another. But Iago obviously goes too far. He not only feels understandable and possibly justified indignation; he also feels downright hatred. He is not satisfied merely to lower his masters Othello and Cassio; he wants to destroy them. Their superiority does not merely irritate him, it maddens him, driving him to acts that are not only vicious but self-destructive. Ordinary social or professional spites do not drive normal people on to murder and self-destruction, and those who, like Iago, cannot control their resentment probably act on motives that are very different from simple anger at their superiors' worldly success.

A deeper source of Iago's hatred of Othello and Cassio lies back of his feeling that the two of them have robbed him of his just deserts. That source reveals itself, a little distortedly perhaps, in the other reason he gives for despising them: his suspicion that they have both committed adultery with Emilia and thus made a cuckold of him. The reader, knowing the suspicion to be preposterous, may think that Iago is not really serious, that he is merely rationalizing his hatred as it were, by giving any reason that comes to mind. But clearly Iago was enough convinced that Emilia and Othello had an affair to have hinted his suspicion to Emilia herself, who alludes to it when, guessing that someone has lied to Othello about Desdemona's chastity, she says:

> Some such squire he was
> That turn'd your wit the seamy side without,
> And made you to suspect me with the Moor,
>
> (IV, ii, 146–148)

A husband who doubts his wife's faithfulness probably suspects that his competitor is sexually his superior, for otherwise the jealous person would have nothing to fear. Whether or not Iago literally believes that Othello and Cassio cuckolded him, his fear that they could have done so has a kind of reasonableness, for in a way that Iago himself seems to feel, they are in fact his superiors sexually, better, more manly than he.

The difference is that whereas Othello's and Cassio's feelings about sex are healthy, Iago's are diseased. Whenever Iago thinks about the relations of men and women his mind immediately runs to images of copulation. Always it is the mechanism of the sexual act that intrigues him. Thus he habitually compares humans' sexual lives with those of other animals. Here are the words in which he announces to Brabantio that Othello and Desdemona have eloped:

> Even now, now, very now, an old black ram
> Is tupping your white ewe.
>
> (I, i, 88–89)

A little later when he teases Brabantio with another picture of animalistic love-making (I, i, 110–111)—"You'll have your daughter covered with a Barbary horse"—and Brabantio asks with astonishment, "What profane wretch art thou?" (114), Iago cannot forego another animal connection with sex (115–117): "I am one, sir, that comes to tell you, your daughter and the Moor are now making the beast with two backs." By contrast, Roderigo's taunts are much less lubricious, even though he also wants to sting Brabantio. He announces (126) that Desdemona has been carried off "To the gross clasps of a lascivious Moor,"—that she has "made a gross revolt." Whereas Roderigo's language expresses moral outrage, only alluding to physical details, Iago's revels in lurid pictures of the sexual act itself.

Iago's preoccupation with the mechanical side of sexual acts is a very different thing from the licentiousness that frequently crops up in Elizabethan plays. The difference is illustrated in *Othello,* for instance, by contrasting Iago's genuinely obsessive speeches concerning sex, with the speeches of the clown, at the beginning of the third act, which are merely indecent and, to our modern feelings, nasty. Iago compulsively dwells upon his images of sex so that, in the third and fourth acts, when he tries to convince Othello of Desdemona's infidelity, the pictures that come to his mind are again those of unrestrained animal intercourse. He tells Othello that he could not show Desdemona and Cassio actually making love, even

> Were they as prime as goats, as hot as monkeys,
> As salt as wolves in pride.

> (III, iii, 404–405)

And Iago's fabrication of Cassio's words and acts in a dream, which Iago says Cassio had when the two slept together, is all a doting litany of physical pleasures (III, iii, 414–427). Iago broods over these erotic sensations and deliberately prolongs them with descriptive evocation; they impart great pleasure, it seems, but also a yearning pain. They are pornographic, not humorous. The clown's images, on the other hand, are ridiculous and therefore funny because they shock but give no pleasure that we are willing to entertain for long. They surprise us first, by insinuating into our minds a picture that we ordinarily repress; then, when we recognize the picture for what it is, we reject it with an embarrassed laugh. The clown's speeches, based on infantile sexuality, are absurd, whereas Iago's salacious remarks, belonging to a later stage of development which we have less perfectly outgrown, are frightening.

Basically, Iago's trouble with sex is that he has not developed beyond boyhood's obsession with anatomical details and physical operations. Most grown men can remember, though they would rather forget, a time when they themselves were preoccupied with these things and rarely thought of women in any other way—and indeed it is possible occasionally for anyone to revert to the earlier stage, as Cassio does for once in the rancid display of machismo which Iago tricks him into when they talk about Bianca (Act IV, Scene I) and as Othello does also, more terribly, throughout the last three acts.

Nonetheless, Cassio's sexual feelings and, in the first part of the play, Othello's too are basically healthy and romantic; Iago's are basically unhealthy and prurient. Shakespeare sharply contrasts them on this point. In Act II, Scene 3, just before Cassio begins drinking more wine than is good for him, he and Iago have this conversation about Desdemona, which Iago tries to push toward salacity and which Cassio repeatedly turns to innocent admiration.

> Cas: Welcome, Iago; we must to the watch.
>
> Iago: Not this hour, lieutenant; 'tis not yet ten o' the clock.
> Our general [Othello] cast us thus early for the love
> of his Desdemona; who let us not therefore blame: he hath
> not yet made wanton the night with her; and she is sport
> for Jove.
>
> Cas: She's a most exquisite lady.
>
> Iago: And, I'll warrant her, full of game.
>
> Cas: Indeed, she is a most fresh and delicate creature.
>
> Iago: What an eye she has! Methinks it sounds a parley to
> provocation.
>
> Cas: An inviting eye; and yet methinks right modest.
>
> Iago: And when she speaks, is it not an alarum to love?
>
> Cas: She is indeed perfection.
>
> (II, iii, 12–28)

Iago does not dare to use such suggestive language to Othello until later in the play, after Othello's degeneration has progressed, and even then it is Iago who offers vivid imagery of copulating bodies, Othello who generally represses it. Near the beginning of Act IV Othello asks Iago if Cassio has bragged of having possessed Desdemona.

> Oth: Hath he said anything?
>
> Iago: He hath, my lord; but be you well assur'd,
> No more than he'll unswear.
>
> Oth: What hath he said?
>
> Iago: Faith, that he did—I know not what he did.
>
> Oth: What? what?
>
> Iago: Lie—
>
> Oth: With her?
>
> Iago: With her, on her, what you will.
>
> (IV, i, 29–34)

Iago's changing of the conventional expression "lie with her" to the more explicitly pictorial "lie on her" characterizes his compulsive voyeurism, his infantile preoccupation with *seeing* sexual acts.

The foregoing interpretation of Iago's character would come as no surprise to Iago himself, not, at any rate, by the end of the drama. Early in the play Iago had attributed his hatred of Cassio to the suspicion that Cassio had committed adultery with Emilia, but by the end he knows better. When considering the necessity of killing Cassio, Iago says to himself:

> If Cassio do remain,
> He hath a daily beauty in his life
> That makes me ugly; and, besides, the Moor
> May unfold me to him; there stand I in much peril.
> No, he must die.

(V, i, 18–22)

The sensible fear that Othello and Cassio may come to an understanding and thus realize that Iago has deceived them both is given in these lines as only the second reason for dispatching Cassio. The first reason is that "he hath a daily beauty in his life" which, in comparison, makes Iago "ugly." Two degrees in Iago's sense of inferiority emerge here. The words *beauty* and *ugly* suggest Iago's insecurity about his appearance, an insecurity that characterizes an immature level of psychosexual development, in males at least. But the words *daily* and *life* show where Iago's main envy of the other men lies. Both Cassio and Othello, who is not physically attractive, have a "daily beauty" in the way they live, a fineness of deportment that arises from noble feelings which a man ought to have if he is to be manly in either an ethical or a psychological sense. Until Iago tampers with them, Othello and Cassio do not even dream of harboring ignoble thoughts about a woman. Iago will harbor such thoughts, but he knows that his lubricity is a flaw, not an increment, in the manliness that is so important to him. One of the maxims of the Duke de la Rochefoucauld runs, "L'hypocrisie, c'est l'hommage que le vice rend à la vertue." Rochefoucauld might as well have said that in some cases at least, hatred is the homage that vice pays to virtue.

So, then, Iago's fundamental reason for hating Othello and Cassio is that they are more manly than he is. Of course he does not plainly say that. Few would. Our own sexuality is so closely implicated with our selves and our sense of our own worth that hardly any of us will directly face the thought that some other person is more manly or more womanly than himself or herself. What Iago does is to express his fear ambiguously, in a proposition that both vents the fundamental cause of his hatred of the two others and at the same time conceals it from his own conscious recognition. He complains that they may have seduced Emilia; underneath that complaint lies his envious belief that they could have seduced her because they are better men, precisely as men, than he is.

With respect to Iago's suspicion that Othello has corrupted Emilia, a perfectly appropriate, symmetrical revenge would be for Iago to seduce

Desdemona. Indeed, at one point this idea does enter his mind. In part of a soliloquy in Act II in which Iago examines his own motives (like most neurotics, Iago is inveterately self-analytical), he says:

> The Moor, howbeit that I endure him not,
> Is of a constant, loving, noble nature,
> And I dare think he'll prove to Desdemona
> A most dear husband. Now, I do love her too;
> Not out of absolute lust,—though peradventure
> I stand accountant for as great a sin,—
> But partly led to diet my revenge,
> For that I do suspect the lusty Moor
> Hath leap'd into my seat; the thought whereof
> Doth like a poisonous mineral gnaw my inwards;
> And nothing can or shall content my soul
> Till I am even'd with him, wife for wife.

(II, i, 291–302)

(The epithet "lusty Moor" betrays Iago's fascination with Othello's sexuality and, perhaps, a suspicion that it exceeds his own.) But the idea of seducing Desdemona only fleets through Iago's mind, never to return. In rejecting this form of revenge, Iago may show that he does not take altogether seriously his fear that Othello has made a cuckold of him. In the next lines, as Iago's thought comes closer to the vengeance that he finally takes, he also approaches more nearly his basic reason for hating Othello as his superior in masculinity.

> Or failing so, yet that I put the Moor
> At least into a jealousy so strong
> That judgment cannot cure.

(303–305)

Othello must be made to be even worse in at least one point of character, manly trust, than Iago himself. As this first tentative notion takes on a more definite shape in the last three acts, it comes to center first on arousing Othello's jealousy; but later, after convincing Othello that Desdemona has been unfaithful, Iago refines the original plan and strives to debase Othello so that the two of them become still more alike, particularly in their thoughts about sex.

The degree of success which Iago achieves in degrading Othello can be seen by comparing typical speeches that occur early in the play with some that come later. In the first act, Othello asks the Venetian senate to allow Desdemona to accompany him to Cyprus, and both his meaning and his way of expressing it bespeak the loftiness, the spiritual grandeur, that makes Desdemona say, "I saw Othello's visage in his mind" (I, iii, 253). Here is how Othello makes his request:

> Vouch with me, heaven, I therefore beg it not

To please the palate of my appetite,
Nor to comply with heat,—the young affects
In me defunct,—and proper satisfaction,
But to be free and bounteous to her mind;
And heaven defend your good souls that you think
I will your serious and great business scant
When she is with me.

(I, iii, 262–269)

And in the second act the greeting between him and Desdemona when they rejoin each other in Cyprus after a dangerous voyage has the high-mindedness that transforms sexual desire into romantic love.

Oth. O my fair warrior!

Des. My dear Othello!

Oth. It gives me wonder great as my content
To see you here before me. O my soul's joy!
If after every tempest come such calms,
May the winds blow till they have waken'd death!
And let the labouring bark climb hills of seas
Olympus-high, and duck again as low
As hell's from heaven! If it were now to die,
'Twere now to be most happy, for I fear
My soul hath her content so absolute
That not another comfort like to this
Succeeds in unknown fate.

Des. The heavens forbid
But that our loves and comforts should increase
Even as our days do grow!

Oth. Amen to that, sweet powers!
I cannot speak enough of this content;
It stops me here; it is too much of joy.
And this, and this, the greatest discords be *(kissing her)*
That e'er our hearts shall make!

(II, i, 182–199)

After the beginning of the third act and before the last scene, nearly any speech by Othello is the opposite of the peaceful loftiness of the lines above. His talk reveals a radical transformation of character. In the fourth act (i, 34–43) he gibbers:

Lie with her! Lie on her! We say, lie on her, when they belie her. Lie with her! Zounds, that's fulsome. Handkerchief,—confessions,—handkerchief! To confess, and be hanged for his labour. First, to be hanged, and then to confess: I tremble at it. Nature would not invest herself in such shadowing passion without some instruction. It is not words that shake me thus. Pish! Noses, ears, and lips. Is it possible?—Confess!—Handkerchief!—O devil!

(IV, i, 35–43)

In an earlier scene he talks nastiness:

> I had been happy, if the general camp,
> Pioners and all, had tasted her sweet body,
> So I had nothing known.

                            (III, iii, 346-348)

Elsewhere in the third act, third scene, he threatens and blusters: "Death and damnation! O!" (397), "I'll tear her all to pieces" (432), "O! blood, blood, blood!" (452), "Damn her, lewd minx! O, damn her!" (476).

Insecurely possessing his own manhood, Iago finds himself mocked in Othello's rich virility, so he wants to destroy the thing that in comparison belittles him. He succeeds so well in his ambition that at the nadir of Othello's moral degeneration, even his language loses its habitual grandeur and imitates Iago's low speech. Othello's exclamation "goats and monkeys," which he makes when he hears Desdemona explain to Lodovico the estrangement between Cassio and himself (IV, i, 265), mimics Iago's earlier obscene remark that he could not show Desdemona and Cassio having intercourse even if they were "as prime as goats, as hot as monkeys." Othello's abasement goes so far that in the last three acts the tone of his thought and feeling is on a level with Iago's. He puts the lowest possible construction on innocent acts and inflames his mind with sexual images. He sinks to eavesdropping and at last to commissioning and committing murder.

Who in this tragedy is most wrong? Iago, who might have been redeemed from his own lowness had he generously loved the good in Othello rather than envied it? Othello, who, much less high-minded than he thought he was and than his position required him to be, submitted finally to gross impulses? A modern reader will hesitate to answer these delicate casuistic questions of guilt. Perhaps Shakespeare's audience delighted in the assurance that Iago would be tortured, but we do not, for the intervening centuries have taught us to be less confident about moral judgment than our ancestors apparently were. But an audience that has lived through the dreadful experience of this play must realize that it deals with a fact of the moral life that is much more basic than guilt or innocence: It is the fact that at best we only hold on to our humanity with our finger tips.

Teaching the Play

The Teacher's Preparation

There exist so many good editions of Shakespeare, suited to different uses, that selection of a particular one depends largely on the reader's purpose and taste. For the teacher who wants informative critical and historical notes,

G. L. Kitteridge's editions can be recommended. These are *Complete Works of Shakespeare* (Boston: Ginn and Company, 1936) and *The Tragedy of Othello, the Moor of Venice* (Boston: Ginn and Company, 1941). As for criticism, still a highly valuable approach to Shakespeare is A. C. Bradley's *Shakespearean Tragedy: Lectures on Hamlet, Othello, King Lear, Macbeth* (London: Macmillan Company, 1st ed. 1894, frequently reprinted). The teacher will profit from reading not only the chapter on *Othello* but also the book's first two chapters, which deal with the substance and the construction of Shakespearean tragedy. Bradley approaches Shakespeare from a philosophical, even a metaphysical, point of view. By contrast, the stagecraft of *Othello* receives illuminating study in Harley Granville-Barker, *Prefaces to Shakespeare* (Princeton, N.J.: Princeton University Press, 1946), IV, 120–266. A collection of notable essays on *Othello,* ranging in time from Thomas Rymer's ferocious attack (1693) to work written in the 1950s, is available in Leonard F. Dean, ed., *A Casebook on Othello* (New York: Thomas Y. Crowell Company, 1961). Robert B. Heilman offers a thorough study, especially attentive to image clusters, in *Magic Web: Action and Language in Othello* (Lexington: University of Kentucky Press, 1956). The teacher can select any one of the many strands of imagery which Heilman indicates (Iago as thief, for instance), offer students one or two clues of it, and then ask them to follow it out through the work. The book by Kenneth Tynan, ed., *Othello: The National Theatre Production* (London: Rupert Hart-Davis Limited, 1966; New York: Stein and Day, 1967) is described below.

Teaching the Idea of Tragedy

Students do not need a highly technical or theoretical idea of the nature of tragedy, but in order to understand *Othello* they do need to know what to expect, for without some preliminary notion of what the play will be like, they are prone to misconstrue it and thus to respond to it irrelevantly. The essential feature of tragedy seems to be a quality that can be called the awful, the terrible, or the dreadful—the consciousness that, for a moment at least, a life has broken out beyond the boundaries that usually confine it and has entered into a scheme of things normally foreign to humans. The reason tragic heroes and heroines die is that, having learned of a spiritual realm in which customary human usages have no place, they are no longer suited to the life of ordinary mortals. But their dying is not the thing that makes a tragedy, which essentially is neither sad nor happy, but terrific.

Examples can help students to grasp this distinction. Willa Cather's "Paul's Case," if the class has read it, can illustrate the difference between sadness and tragedy. Paul's death is sad because it cuts off a life that has never been fulfilled. But it is not tragic, for Paul lives and dies in this world of human affairs. To be sure, he fantasizes about a dream world of extreme comfort and high style, but the world he imagines is not another, different world; it is still merely Pittsburgh with deluxe accommodations. With Othello the case is altogether different. In the last scene, just after the point of maximum sorrow where Othello finally becomes convinced that Desdemona has been true to him and that in murdering her he has destroyed all hope of happiness, there comes to him the serenity of his final speech. All at once he has been visited by an intuition of an order of things so different from his own turbulence that his rage suddenly ends and he dies in a calm of spirit that exists for us only in tragedy—both literary and real—and in religion. (Tragedy and religion both deal with our intimations of a terrific "other," but tragedy is predominantly personal and private, religion primarily social and institutional.)

Introducing the Play

Ordinarily we detest the use of plot summaries, for the good reason that a summary is a very different thing from the plot itself and far inferior to it. But a Shakespearean play is exceptional. In the play there are so many obstacles to understanding—in the language, metaphors, ideas, versification, characters—that the reader needs as a minimum to know what is going on in order to give full attention to these other features. With no subplot and a very direct line of action, the plot of *Othello* can be briefly summarized. The teacher can either read to students or hand them such an outline as this:

> Othello, a Moor who has been converted to Christianity, has been so successful a general for the Venetians that he has won great acclaim and trust in that country. At the beginning of the play he has just secretly married Desdemona, the beautiful daughter of the senator Brabantio, who, outraged that his daughter should marry a man who is both a foreigner and a black, complains to his fellow senators that Othello has seduced her by using witchcraft. Desdemona assures the senators that true love, not witchcraft, has led to the marriage, and she wins her argument.
>
> At the time when this dispute takes place, news arrives that the Turkish fleet is about to attack Cyprus, a Venetian island colony in the eastern Mediterranean. The senate gives Othello command, and he immediately leaves for Cyprus with an army. In a different ship, Desdemona also departs, accompanied by Iago, Othello's trusted but treacherous subordinate, and by Iago's wife, Emilia, who will act as Desdemona's lady-in-waiting.
>
> Iago, who hates Othello, begins to shape a plan for undoing him. Once arrived in Cyprus, Iago quickly persuades Othello that Desdemona is having an affair with a young officer, Cassio. Enraged, Othello attempts to cause Cassio's death and succeeds in murdering Desdemona, only moments before he receives clear evidence that Iago has deceived him. In despair Othello kills himself.

After giving students this summary, a teacher would ideally go on to present *Othello* in a complete performance, preferably live or at least filmed. Few teachers, however, will be able to make this provision, and most teachers will have to fall back on other alternatives. They have a consolation: Even though Shakespeare was a performer who wrote for the live theater, he was also a major poet, constructing works that repay the close study that comes from reading and not just seeing and hearing. The proof that he did not regard himself as merely another playwright turning out scripts is that he left so-called acting versions and also full, literary texts for many of the plays.

Luckily, *Othello* has been recorded a number of times. There are two fine recordings, each giving a different view of Othello's character—one by Laurence Olivier (RCA Victor VDS 100) and one by Paul Robeson (Columbia SL 153). If the teacher wishes, one of the recordings can be played straight through during a succession of classes, with the students following the dialogue in their texts. Although this procedure has some obvious advantages, it also has a drawback in that it chops up the flow of the play into discontinuous segments.

There may be a better way of helping students to involve themselves deeply in *Othello*—that is, by reading the play within a short time span, over a weekend perhaps. The teacher, having already helped the students by providing a plot synopsis, can help them further by giving some practical advice about how best to read *Othello* the first time. They can be told that this play gets its effect in part by its fast-paced action when the scene shifts to Cyprus. In their first reading the students can keep up with this pace if they concentrate on grasping the characters' feelings and actions without worrying much about the exact significance of individual words. As an example, here is Othello telling the Venetian senators that he likes an active life and is therefore eager to begin his campaign against the Turks:

> The tyrant custom, most grave senators,
> Hath made the flinty and steel couch of war
> My thrice-driven bed of down: I do agnize
> A natural and prompt alacrity
> I find in hardness, and do undertake
> These present wars against the Ottomites.

(I, iii, 229–234)

If the student realizes that searching out the meanings of words in this intricately expressed passage is not nearly as important as sensing the kind of man Othello is—a man who loves both order and grandness—then that student will be encouraged to go on with the reading, knowing that it is possible to understand what is essential in a passage like this one even though some of the expressions are baffling. Here is another fine speech of Othello's which, even if many of the words are unfamiliar, nevertheless conveys a vivid impression of the dauntless adventurer. Othello tells of being invited by Brabantio, Desdemona's father, to come to his house and tell of his past life:

> Her father lov'd me; oft invited me;
> Still question'd me the story of my life
> From year to year, the battles, sieges, fortunes
> That I have pass'd.
> I ran it through, even from my boyish days
> To the very moment that he bade me tell it;
> Wherein I spoke of most disastrous chances,
> Of moving accidents by flood and field,
> Of hair-breadth 'scapes i' the imminent deadly breach,
> Of being taken by the insolent foe
> And sold to slavery, of my redemption thence
> And portance in my travel's history;
> Wherein of antres vast and deserts idle,
> Rough quarries, rocks, and hills whose heads touch heaven,
> It was my hint to speak, such was my process;
> And of the Cannibals that each other eat,
> The Anthropophagi, and men whose heads
> Do grow beneath their shoulders.
>
> (I, iii, 128–145)

The reader need not worry over the meaning that *imminent* is supposed to convey in the phrase "imminent deadly breach" nor bother about the source of those "men whose heads do grow beneath their shoulders." (Shakespeare got them from a medieval book called *Travels of Sir John Mandeville.*) What can be grasped easily, and what is more important to know, is that Othello has the makings of a poet, the love of splendor in things and words—and is thus all the more defenseless against Iago's lowness of feeling, which is incomprehensible to him until he is finally sucked into it.

In class the teacher can read or play on the phonograph these two speeches and others like them—for instance, Othello's assertion that he will never change his mind (III, iii, 454–461)—and these readings will show the students that the passages become meaningful when they are taken as wholes, and that individual words which we cannot understand when we see them standing alone gain significance as we allow them to take their natural place in the surging, musical, almost operatic, flow of Othello's grand declamations. The language of the play will become much simpler for students as they hear it read aloud, either by the teacher or by fellow students who have carefully prepared themselves. Gradually the characteristic rhythms of this play—the grand, sweeping surge of Othello's speeches, the softer and more various cadences of Desdemona's passages, Iago's staccato utterances—will make themselves heard and will convey a fuller emotional meaning than the words by themselves can express.

The Assignment

The teacher hopes that the students will be able to concentrate their attention
very sharply on the play as they read it, and will try to make the assignment
in ways that aid this concentration. An interesting visual dimension can be
added to the students' reading of the play if the teacher obtains a copy of
Tynan's *Othello: The National Theatre Production*. This book contains a
number of arresting insights into the play (by F. R. Leavis and W. H. Auden,
among others) and also has a large collection of photographs which should
help a reader to constitute the characters and settings. This book can be a
basis for exercises in constituting if the teacher shows some of the pictures
and asks such questions as: "Does this photograph resemble the character
that exists in your mind?" "Do you know of other performers who resemble
the character more closely?" "Does the clothing correspond with your idea of
the character's dress?" (A student may notice that, in the production which
this book documents, Othello is dressed in richly colored, heavy, voluminous
robes in the first two acts, when his dignity and self-command are uppermost,
whereas later in the play, as his character degenerates, his clothing becomes
scantier and, at last, flimsy.) "Do the characters' gestures, facial expressions,
and posture as they speak certain lines agree with your conception?" Perfect
agreement on these questions is not to be expected. Different readers of the
play will of course constitute it somewhat differently, for reasons that were
dealt with in Chapter II. In fact these differences should encourage the
teacher, for they will show that the students are constituting the play—
making it exist—and also that they are building up a reservoir of possible
responses, out of which different readers can select the ones that make the
play credible and interesting to them.

There is an assignment, fairly easy to fulfill, that will help the students to
read dialogue as a clue to character. Students are asked to take about six
continuous lines from one of Othello's speeches in the first or second act, and
about the same number of lines from a speech by Iago in either of those same
acts, and then determine what the talk of each man reveals about his
character. If a student needs help in finding appropriate passages, the teacher
can point out some. In Act I, Scene iii, Othello commences a speech to the
Venetian senators in which he justifies himself for marrying Desdemona.
These lines which open that speech show his delight in decorous, slightly
orotund language that asserts dignity and self-possession:

> Most potent, grave, and reverend signiors,
> My very noble and approv'd good masters,
> That I have ta'en away this old man's daughter,
> It is most true; true I have married her:
> The very head and front of my offending
> Hath this extent, no more.

> (I, iii, 76–81)

Here, by contrast, is Iago in a speech at the end of Act I, spluttering out his contempt for the simpleton Roderigo, whom he is about to bilk, and his hatred of Othello. The speech seems harsh and clipped when it is compared with the slower pace and expansive utterance in Othello's passage above.

> Thus do I ever make my fool my purse;
> For I my own gain'd knowledge should profane,
> If I would time expend with such a snipe
> But for my sport and profit. I hate the Moor,
> And it is thought abroad that 'twixt my sheets
> He has done my office.

(I, iii, 382–387)

At the time when the teacher makes this part of the assignment, the students can also be advised to watch for the sharply different ways in which Othello, Cassio, and Iago talk and feel about women.

Another way in which the teacher can help the students to read *Othello* more closely is to suggest that the story might have turned out differently had certain characters not behaved as they did at certain points in the action. An example is Desdemona's eager intercession for Cassio, a kindness which Othello misconstrues as a sign of adulterous love. The students can then be alert for other moments when characters behave in ways that lead to the outcome. They may notice that Desdemona does not tell the whole truth in her answer to Othello's question about the handkerchief, and they may see that a completely frank answer from her at this point might have prepared Othello to resist Iago's imputation that Desdemona gave it to Cassio. Or they may observe that the handkerchief would never have been lost at all had not Othello complained, dishonestly, that he had a headache. Cassio's one lapse into drunkenness is another instance of an event which, had it turned out otherwise, would have led to a different denouement. In the class discussion of these episodes the point ought to arise that, although there is some element of chance involved in the characters' behavior, still they act in ways that are probable for them to have acted. Cassio might well have allowed himself a glass of wine in just those particular circumstances: new people around him, a promotion that makes him feel good about himself, Iago's flattery and coaxing. Similarly, Desdemona stretches the truth when she says the handkerchief is not lost, but that is the sort of "white lie" that is often told.

Shakespeare's handling of time in this play is intriguing, and the students, if their teacher gives them some preliminary hints, may be able to discover the details of it in their first reading. During the first act, the stage time and the depicted time are identical or nearly so. In the last four acts, however, the depicted time seems to progress at two different rates of speed. Clearly the sequence of action is rapid: There is the landing at Cyprus, the dinner and mounting the guard, the quarrel late at night, Iago's talk the next day with Cassio and Othello, the attempt that night to murder Cassio, and the killing of Desdemona at about the same time. At this pace all the action, from the landing on Cyprus to the end of the play, can be encompassed in a period of thirty-six hours or somewhat less. Nevertheless, at the end of the play we feel as if a considerable amount of time has elapsed. Certain speeches give us this impression. Emilia's remark that Iago has often asked her to steal the handkerchief that Othello gave Desdemona (III, iii, 292–293) makes little sense unless we presume that all the characters had been on Cyprus for some time; before then, Iago's scheme had not matured to the point where he needed it to be. Moreover, Bianca's reproach to Cassio, "What! Keep a week away? seven days and nights?" (III, iv, 171), though it could possibly refer to an earlier period in Venice, more naturally suggests that Cassio has been avoiding her in the recent past on Cyprus.

These two different impressions of the flow of time support two different feelings, both of which are needed if the play is to exert its full impact. The slower of the two schedules increases probability, for Othello's raging jealousy is more credible if we imagine that Iago had a certain length of time to build it up. The rapid development, which seems to predominate in our minds over the slow one, places the conclusion of the action within a day-and-a-half of the characters' arrival at Cyprus, and thus, through the suddenness of events, it makes the disaster all the more overwhelming, and it also emphasizes the underlying instability of Othello's character, the instability that paved the way for his transformation.

Class Discussion

If the teacher has given a sufficiently detailed assignment, when the students come back to class from their reading of *Othello* they should have much that they can profitably discuss. Some of the questions and hints that were given in the assignment can be taken up in the classroom. For instance, the students may want to compare their visual constitutings of the different characters or to consider the ways in which characters' actions lead to the outcome of the drama. This discussion may proceed to related points. Someone may insist that, although the whole sequence of events makes Othello's final acts psychologically possible or even probable, still those acts are not necessary—a distinction that other students may want to challenge.

In addition, the classroom work can bring up new material. The teacher can point out some crucial lines and then ask what presentation these lines can have. Othello's "Put out the light, and then put out the light:" (V, ii, 7) can be read with a wide variety of stresses so as to make different suggestions.

For instance, very different effects can be obtained by putting the heaviest stress on any one of the words that appear after the comma. The murder scene that begins with this line can be paced at different speeds. (For my own part, I prefer it to move more rapidly than I have seen done in stage presentations.) If the students can be got to discuss such matters as these in order to find out what different constitutings are possible, they may find themselves giving dramatic delivery to the lines and perhaps even miming some of the action without embarrassment. They will have become involved with technical problems of realization and production, much as a professional actor does.

Another light is cast on the play when one sees what alterations Shakespeare made in his source. A convenient, short summary of Cinthio's original version can be found in Dean's *A Casebook on Othello*. If the teacher reads this summary aloud, the students will be able to detect the changes which Shakespeare made, and they will also have ideas as to his reasons for them.

Closing the Unit

Up to this point in their study of *Othello* the students have received various kinds of helpful preparation from the teacher, they have read the play through one time, and they have discussed their readings with each other, to correct their views and also to learn of possible responses which they themselves did not make in their own initial readings. Now it is time for them to go back to the play for another reading, which will be both more intense and more accurate because of all this preliminary work.

This second, better reading, like the earlier one, needs guidance, and the teacher can now make alternative assignments to direct the rereading so that still more sharing by the students can take place. Some students can be asked to read the play and at the same time listen to one of the recordings. They can see what lines were cut in the recorded production, and they can give their opinion about the justice of the cutting. They can also spot passages that the actors spoke differently from what the students' reading had led them to expect, and they can form an opinion as to which realization of the passage is better. This exercise can lead students to new insight which they can share with the class, probably in oral form.

Still other students can approach their second reading in a different manner, by studying *Othello* to see if they can find answers to some new questions that the teacher will pose for them. Here are some of the questions, which can be divided among small groups of students for their consideration: (1) Can Iago's eagerness to ruin Othello be explained? (2) What features of Othello's character and situation expose him to Iago's plot? (3) Is Othello truly as noble in the first part of the play as he appears to be? (4) How could a skillful actor suggest the flaws that exist in Othello's character? The students' findings can be reported in different ways. In one kind of class, panel discussions, with participation by the class, may succeed. In a different class setting, lectures by individual students may work better. Or, alternatively, the students who examine these questions can write essays for distribution to the class.

If the teacher plans to conclude the unit with writing by the students, the class discussions will reveal plenty of questions and contested points that should serve very well as focal points for essays. Interpretations of Othello's character and of Iago's vary, and so does the apportionment of blame for the tragedy that occurs. Another subject for writing can be almost any one of Othello's speeches, since they are all so rich in allusion, rhythm, and sentiment that even a very few lines can repay close attention. A student who writes about the glamorous line "Keep up your bright swords, for the dew will rust them" (I, ii, 59) can focus the essay on an analysis of the thoughts and feelings that arise as those words flow through the reader's consciousness and what features in the line account for this response. These essays certainly ought to serve a larger purpose than gaining the student credit or giving the teacher evidence for a grade, which are only secondary aims. More importantly, the essays should be a serious part of the class study of *Othello*. They can work in this way if the class is given the opportunity to read them. The essays can be exchanged among students or they can be read aloud, or, better, they can be reproduced and handed out. In any case, they should be discussed, for that discussion will not only ensure an interested audience for the writer—it will also add more layers to the continually expanding awareness which such a masterpiece as *Othello* activates in its readers.

Afterword

The question "What is the best way to teach literature?" is difficult to answer, not because of a lack of information or ideas about the subject of literature but, on the contrary, because of the great number of authenticated literary facts and reliable explanations. For instance, we already know—or can easily discover—the main facts concerning the composition and publication of *Paradise Lost.* In the writing of reliable scholars we have access to enough discerning interpretations of Milton's characterization of Satan to allow us to see that Milton could both abominate and, in a certain sense, admire that great rebel. There is much more about Milton and *Paradise Lost* that we either know or can learn. But when we turn to the matter of teaching *Paradise Lost,* our technical knowledge about that work and about literature in general creates questions without answering them. What age and what level of readiness are necessary for readers before they can appreciate *Paradise Lost?* Can the first two books be taught alone without sacrificing something important? Can the work be taught as a whole but the reading time shortened by the use of synopses? Should students also read some other example of epic literature and, if so, what work? Does a good reading of *Paradise Lost* require explicit knowledge of epic conventions, of Christian theology, of Milton's condition when he wrote it? With modern works the case is the same. If we try to teach Baldwin's *The Fire Next Time* or Vonnegut's *Breakfast of Champions,* questions about teaching those works will arise which our technical information will not suffice to answer.

So, then, when we decide upon ways of teaching a work, we consider not only the work itself but other points as well. We take from our knowledge of the field of the psychology of learning as much as we find useful. In addition, everything we know about our students we try to apply to our teaching. Something else has equal bearing with these considerations on our decisions about the teaching of a work, and that is our idea of the value of literature—of what good it can do for its readers. Having decided what is the good of a literary work, we can then aim to teach works in ways that help students to acquire that good.

Literature must be good for a number of different things, because the fact is that readers make different uses of it. Sometimes we read literature to escape our physical or spiritual environments, and because that escape can involve some measure of self-transcendence, it can be important and not at all trivial. Sometimes we use literature to sharpen our moral discernment.[1] Sometimes we find it to be a source of historical or psychological knowledge. Sometimes literature aids self-discovery, perhaps even self-enhancement. And none of these functions necessarily excludes other uses; the same novel or poem that lifts us out of our immediate world can also return us to that world equipped with new understanding of it.

The question remains, however: What is literature *most* good for? Or—a better way of phrasing the question perhaps—what is it so good for that other uses should be secondary? Although I am willing to admit that the uses of literature as listed above are valuable, they do not seem to me to be the most valuable. I think the best thing that literature does for readers has been implied throughout this book and has been the basis of the recommendations for teaching. But now I ought to discuss this question of value plainly.[2]

What is the good of literature? Like all the arts, it is good for presenting modes of consciousness. It presents the myriad and indescribably intricate shapes which the inner life of a person takes as that life flickers outward to notice things in the world or the self, to think about those things, to reject or embrace them, to will their well-being or their extinction. English no longer has a word to express the effects that this presentation can have on personality, the terms *refined, cultured, sensitive* all having degenerated now into negative and almost mocking suggestions. Years ago, long before the present day when *competence* has become the educational watchword, even before the time when we looked for so-called relevance in everything we taught, teachers valued "maturity" and aimed to produce in their students "the mature mind," to quote the title of a book by Harry Overstreet[3]—a book that was popular in the 'fifties, both within and outside the teaching profession. Perhaps those terms *maturity* and *the mature mind* best describe the effect on personality which literature and the other arts can have by setting forth patterns of consciousness.

The idea of maturity is more easily expressed in examples than in formal definitions. William the Conqueror illustrated what is *not* meant by maturity when, on being introduced to the woman who was to become his wife, he took her by the hair, threw her on the ground, and stamped on her. We think that behavior was undoubtedly immature. But William and the men and women who lived around him would not have agreed; for their repertoire of consciousness did not possess the forms of thinking-feeling-willing about the opposite sex that we have today. Those patterns were invented by the troubadour poets and were extended and purified later by Petrarch and Shakespeare, and they are sustained today by our poets, dramatists, novelists, film script writers, and other artists. At one place on a steep ladder is the eleventh century Norman who did not know what to do with his future wife except to throw her down and kick her; at another place are we ourselves. And the rungs in the ladder are the poets and the other artists who have made our ascent possible.

This growth of human personality that takes place in historical perspective is also visible within the life-cycle of the individual. For instance, young people, delightful though they are, charm us *just as* young people. No one can, with any pleasure, imagine them retaining as adults the same state of maturity that they possess in youth: they would lack the readiness for dealing with all the happenstances of life, for coping with being thirty or forty years old, parents perhaps, teachers themselves some of them, or nurses, business people, citizens. A visit to an elementary school playground, a secondary school lunch room, or even a college dormitory shows that the ten-year-old, the fifteen-year-old, the twenty-year-old, are all only on the road to the goal of maturity, not at the goal. And we who have reached a stage at which we are entrusted with their education are only a little farther along the same road; certainly we do not think that our growth is complete.

It would be absurd to claim that the study of literature or other arts, by itself, confers the mature mind. For one thing, not all students of literature dazzle us with their maturity. For another, various causes, not just one, help people to acquire the full power of reacting to the chances and changes of life—physical maturation, socialization, intellectual development—through study and general experience. But the arts, literature among them, can aid importantly in developing a mature mind. To attain maturity we need every possible resource. We need physical and emotional strength of course; we need the support of others whom we love—family and friends; we need intellect. Besides these we need something more: a supple, broad, finely tuned consciousness. That is the province of art.

NOTES

Chapter 1

1. Columbia Records, BW 80 (X "LP" 38382).

Chapter 2

1. Various writers on aesthetics and on literature deal with the process which is here called "constituting" and which also goes by the names "realization," "concretization," and, rather misleadingly I feel, "performing." The writers I have found most instructive are Jean Paul Sartre and Roman Ingarden in their essays in *Aesthetics,* ed. Harold Osborne (London: Oxford University Press, 1972), pp. 32–38 and 39–54; Richard P. Blackmur, "A Burden for Critics," *The Hudson Review,* I (1948), 170–185, reprinted in *The Problems of Aesthetics: A Book of Readings,* eds. Eliseo Vivas and Murray Krieger (New York: Holt, Rinehart, and Winston, 1953), pp. 418–430; Louise Rosenblatt, *Literature as Exploration,* 3rd ed. (New York: Noble and Noble, 1976), pp. 277–291. See also Rosenblatt's more recent *The Reader, the Text, the Poem: The Transactional Theory of the Literary Work* (Carbondale and Edwardsville, Ill.: Southern Illinois University Press, 1978), especially Chapter IV, "Evoking a Poem." Although I believe that Rosenblatt would accept much of what I have to say about constituting, it is clear that she rejects the notion of the literary work as an object, even as an "intellected object" existing only in the mind.

2. There is a story that Frank Stockton was once a guest at a dinner party where for dessert he was given two mounds of ice cream, one shaped like a lady and one like a tiger. According to the story, he pushed the two forms together before eating them.

3. *The American Scholar.* Emerson not only accepts this notion of constituting: he carries it, much farther than I care to follow him, to the point of selecting in a text those passages which one considers genuinely inspired, and attending closely to those but ignoring the rest. His attitude is appropriate, perhaps even inevitable, for a reader who looks upon literature as one of the humanities, not as an art. Here is the entire passage:

> I would not be hurried by any love of system, by any exaggeration of instincts, to underrate the Book. We all know, that as the human body can be nourished on any food, though it were boiled grass and the broth of shoes, so the human mind can be fed by any knowledge. And great and heroic men have existed who had almost no other information than by the printed page. I only would say that it needs a strong head to bear that diet. One must be an inventor to read well. As the proverb says, "He that would bring home the wealth of the Indies, must carry out the wealth of the Indies." There is then creative reading as well as creative writing. When the mind is braced by labor and invention, the page of whatever book we read becomes luminous with manifold allusion. Every sentence is doubly significant, and the sense of our author is as broad as the

world. We then see, what is always true, that as the seer's hour of vision is short and rare among heavy days and months, so is its record, perchance, the least part of his volume. The discerning will read, in his Plato or Shakespeare, only that least part—only the authentic utterances of the oracles; all the rest he rejects, were it never so many times Plato's and Shakespeare's.

4. For the theological, psychological, and medical interpretations, see, respectively: Max Brod, *Franz Kafka: A Biography,* trans. from 2nd ed. by G. Humphrey Roberts and Richard Winston (1937; rpt. New York: Schoken Books, 1960); Charles Neider, *The Frozen Sea: A Study of Franz Kafka* (1948; rpt. New York: Russell & Russell, 1962); F. Waismann, "A Philosopher Looks at Kafka," *Essays in Criticism,* III, 2 (April 1953), 177–190.

5. Oliver Wendell Holmes, *The Autocrat of the Breakfast-Table* (Boston: Houghton, Mifflin and Company, Riverside Press, 1892), pp. 103–104.

6. In her *Literature as Exploration,* Louise Rosenblatt's comments on this much-disputed question are very illuminating. In particular see pp. 110, 224–226, and 272–273. She examines the same question also in *The Reader, the Text, the Poem,* Chapter V, "The Text: Openness and Constraint." For an argument that vigorously supports the subjective answer to the question, see David Bleich, *Subjective Criticism* (Baltimore and London: Johns Hopkins University Press, 1978).

7. Leavis's assessment of Fielding appears in *The Great Tradition* (1948; rpt. London: Chatto & Windus, 1962), pp. 3–4. Murry's reply is "In Defense of Fielding," *Unprofessional Essays* (London: Jonathan Cape, 1956), pp. 9–52.

Chapter 3

1. In "Poetry for Poetry's Sake," the first essay in *Oxford Lectures on Poetry,* first printed in 1910 and frequently reprinted since then.

2. *A Preface to Paradise Lost* (1942; rpt. London: Oxford University Press, 1959), pp. 85–87. Denis Saurat, *Milton: Man and Thinker* (1925: rpt. New York: Haskell House Publishers, 1970).

3. *The Letters of John Keats,* ed. Hyder Edward Rollins (Cambridge, Mass.: Harvard University Press, 1958), II, 67.

4. Murry's *Studies in Keats* (1930) underwent substantial revisions in 1939, when it appeared as *Studies in Keats: New and Old;* in 1949, *(The Mystery of Keats);* and in 1955, *(Keats).* Taken as a whole, this series of books, along with *Keats and Shakespeare,* illustrates the growth of an accomplished critic's mind as he contemplates one author over many years.

5. *The Well-Wrought Urn: Studies in the Structure of Poetry* (New York: Harcourt, Brace and Company, 1947), p. 16.

6. "Life of John Keats," in *The Keats Circle: Letters and Papers,* ed. Hyder Edward Rollins, 2nd ed. (Cambridge, Mass.: Harvard University Press, 1965), II, 65.

7. *The Finer Tone: Keats' Major Poems* (1953; rpt. Baltimore: Johns Hopkins University Press, 1967), p. 178.

8. "When Shakespeare Wrote the Sonnets," *The Atlantic* (December 1949), 61–67; reprinted in *Shakespeare's Sonnets Dated and Other Essays* (London: Rupert Hart-Davis, 1949), pp. 4–21. For a lively rejoinder to Hotson's argument, see John Middleton Murry, *John Clare and Other Studies* (London: Peter Neville Limited, 1950), pp. 246–252.

9. 1948; rpt. New York: Octagon Books, 1971.

10. Cambridge, Mass.: Harvard University Press, 1936.

11. *PMLA*, 39 (1924), 229–253.

12. New York: Harcourt, Brace and World, 1930.

13. New York: W. W. Norton and Company, 1953.

14. *The Active Universe: Pantheism and the Concept of Imagination in the English Romantic Poets* (London: Athlone Press, 1962).

15. *A Dream of Order: The Medieval Ideal in Nineteenth Century English Literature* (London: Routledge & Kegan Paul, 1971).

16. John Forster, *The Life of Charles Dickens* (New York: Doubleday, Doran and Company, 1928), p. 25.

17. London: Hutchinson & Company.

18. For a vigorous rebuttal of the more sensational aspects of the Deacon-Coleman thesis, see Robert Gittings, *Young Thomas Hardy* (London: Heinemann, 1975), pp. 223–229.

19. 1924; rpt. New York: Harcourt, Brace and Company, 1952.

20. *Practical Criticism: A Study of Literary Judgment* (1929; rpt. London: Routledge & Kegan Paul, 1970).

21. New York: Oxford University Press, 1968.

22. *Poems in Persons: An Introduction to the Psychoanalysis of Literature* (New York: Norton, 1973).

23. *Poems in Persons*, p. 100. Holland notes that the expression is Stanley Edgar Hyman's.

24. Lately Holland has moved on in his theorizing about literature to restore greater authority to the work. See his articles "Unity Identity Text Self," *PMLA*, 90 (1975), 813–822, and "Literary Interpretation and Three Phases of Psychoanalysis," *Critical Inquiry*, 3 (1976), 221–233.

25. This passage occurs early in Keats's letter of 19 February 1818 to John Hamilton Reynolds. *The Letters of John Keats*, I, 231.

26. *Elements of Writing about a Literary Work: A Study of Response to Literature* (Champaign, Ill.: National Council of Teachers of English, 1968).

27. *Hamlet and Oedipus* (1949; rpt. Garden City, New York: Doubleday and Company, 1954).

28. 1929; rpt. New York: Oxford University Press, 1959.

29. *The Life and Works of Edgar Allen Poe: A Psycho-analytical Interpretation,* trans. John Rodker (London: Imago Publishing Company, 1949).

30. In *Out of My System: Psychoanalysis, Ideology, and Critical Method* (New York: Oxford University Press, 1975), pp. 42–62.

31. London: Oxford University Press, 1934.

32. *Willa Cather,* University of Minnesota Pamphlets on American Writers, No. 7 (Minneapolis: University of Minnesota Press, 1964).

33. *An End to Innocence* (Boston: Beacon Press, 1955), p. 146.

34. In Morton W. Bloomfield, ed., *In Search of Literary Theory* (Ithaca, N.Y., and London: Cornell University Press, 1972), pp. 91–193. Frye's original book of literary theory, still very illuminating as well as controversial, is *Anatomy of Criticism: Four*

Essays (Princeton, N.J.: Princeton University Press, 1957). Though absorbing, the book is long and intricately argued, and readers who find it heavy going may prefer Frye's more sprightly and more simply written book, *The Literary Imagination* (Bloomington, Ind.: Indiana University Press, 1964).

35. In *In Search of Literary Theory,* p. 190.

36. *Exile's Return: A Literary Odyssey of the 1920's* (1934; rpt. New York: Viking Press, 1963).

37. Garden City, New York: Doubleday and Company, 1940.

38. *Axel's Castle: A Study in the Imaginative Literature of 1870–1930* (1931; rpt. New York: Charles Scribner's Sons, 1950).

39. *On Native Grounds: An Interpretation of Modern American Prose Literature* (1942; abridged as Doubleday Anchor Book A69, Garden City, N.Y.: Doubleday, 1956). A more recent book of Kazin's, dealing with American writers since the 'forties, is *Bright Book of Life* (New York: Dell, 1974).

40. Though Communists, both these men have too fine a rationality to be consistent party-liners. The tenor of Lukács' voluminous writing may be represented by his *The Meaning of Contemporary Realism,* trans. John and Necke Mander (London: Merlin Press, 1963), which contains a closely reasoned criticism of "Modernism" as represented by such writers as Kafka and Joyce. Much of Christopher Caudwell's pungent writing has been brought together in *The Concept of Freedom,* ed. George Thomson (London: Lawrence & Wishart, 1965), which collects parts of three of his books. His posthumous book, *Romance and Realism: A Study in English Bourgeois Literature,* is edited by Samuel Hynes (Princeton, N.J.: Princeton University Press, 1970). Both these editions contain remarks on Caudwell by the editors.

Chapter 4

1. *Principles of Literary Criticism,* p. 107.

2. "Milton," in *The Lives of the English Poets,* The World's Classics (London: Oxford University Press, 1959), I, 127.

3. James Boswell, *The Life of Samuel Johnson,* Oxford Standard Authors (London: Oxford University Press, 1966), p. 1309.

4. Henry Thoreau, *Walden,* "The Bean Field."

5. *Aesthetics: Problems in the Philosophy of Criticism* (New York: Harcourt, Brace and Company, 1958), p. 126.

6. *Advice to a Prophet and Other Poems* (New York: Harcourt, Brace and World, 1961), p. 27.

Chapter 5

1. *English Journal,* 55 (January 1966), 39–45, 68; rpt. in *Teaching English in Today's High Schools: Selected Readings,* 2nd ed., eds. Dwight L. Burton and John S. Simmons (New York: Holt, Rinehart and Winston, 1970).

2. *The Way It Spozed to Be* (New York: Simon and Shuster, 1968) and *How to Survive in Your Native Land* (New York: Simon and Shuster, 1971).

3. As far as I can trace this plot scheme, it derives from Gustave Freytag, "Chapter II: The Construction of the Drama," in Freytag's *Technique of the Drama: An*

Exposition of Dramatic Composition and Art, 2nd ed. from the German 6th ed., ed. and trans. Elias J. MacEwan (Chicago: S. C. Griggs and Company, 1896). Although this book, never reprinted I think, is hard to come by outside university libraries, the teacher who reads Chapter II will find a great help in its incisive and intelligible treatment of plotting.

4. And yet a credible argument can be made for including in the curriculum enough information about literary technique to allow students to admire a writer's artistry. This argument has a forceful presentation in Sydney Bolt and Roger Gard, *Teaching Fiction in Schools* (London: Hutchinson Educational Limited, 1970).

Chapter Six

1. See his sonnet "On the Grasshopper and Cricket."

2. See Aileen Ward, *John Keats: The Making of a Poet* (New York: Viking Press, 1963), pp. 30-32 and 66-68, for a sensitive explanation of familial symbols in "Imitation of Spenser" and "Calidore." Miss Ward shows that in those poems water represents the maternal element, but I consider the image of earth in "To Autumn" to carry the same idea.

3. In *The Visionary Company* (Garden City, New York: Doubleday & Company, 1961), p. 423, Harold Bloom notices the sexual imagery of the first stanza, but he does not take it as central to the poem.

4. "Conspire": literally "to breathe together."

5. John Middleton Murry, *Keats and Shakespeare* (1925; rpt. London: Oxford University Press, 1965).

6. *The Letters of John Keats,* II, 101.

7. *The Letters of John Keats,* II, 167. This is the letter of 22 September 1819. Here is the relevant passage: "How beautiful the season is now—How fine the air. A temperate sharpness about it. Really, without joking, chaste weather—Dian skies—I never lik'd stubble fields so much as now—Aye better than the chilly green of the Spring. Somehow a stubble-field looks warm—in the same way that some pictures look warm—this struck me so much in my Sunday's walk that I composed upon it."

Chapter Seven

1. (London: Hamish Hamilton, 1961), p. 198.

Chapter Eight

1. His attachment to Mary Jane Wilks is possibly an exception, but she is much less passively admiring than the other bourgeois women in the novels, much more her own woman.

2. A readily available and fully annotated translation of *Fear and Trembling* and *The Sickness Unto Death* is by Walter Lowrie (Garden City, New York: Doubleday Anchor Books, 1954). Page references in this chapter are to that edition.

3. Tom had suggested that he, Huck, and Jim go to the Indian Territory for "a couple of weeks" of "howling adventures."

4. Lionel Trilling's profound and beautifully written essay can be found as the introduction to the Rinehart edition of *Huckleberry Finn* and also in Trilling's

frequently reprinted *The Liberal Imagination* and in Guy A. Cardwell's *Discussions of Mark Twain.*

Chapter Nine

1. My source for *Othello* throughout this chapter is the Oxford University Press edition (1912; reprinted 1966) edited by W. J. Craig.

Afterword

1. A persuasive account of how literature helps readers to form and refine moral values is Maxine Greene's "Literature and Human Understanding," *The Journal of Aesthetic Education,* 2, No. 4 (October 1968), 11–22, reprinted in Ralph A. Smith, ed., *Aesthetics and Problems of Education* (Urbana: University of Illinois Press, 1971), pp. 200–212.

2. My discussion of the function of art relies upon the writings of Suzanne K. Langer. The reader who wants a succinct statement of Mrs. Langer's point of view can go to the essay "Expressiveness" in her *Problems of Art: Ten Philosophical Lectures* (New York: Charles Scribner's Sons, 1957).

3. Harry Allen Overstreet, *The Mature Mind* (New York: W. W. Norton, 1949).

Author

Bruce E. Miller is associate professor of instruction at State University of New York at Buffalo, where he teaches in the English education program. He received his doctorate in English from the University of Michigan. His publications consist mainly of literary criticism and of articles on the teaching of composition and of literature, and his teaching experience includes work with students from the early secondary through the university graduate years.